HOW TO
MEDITATE
LIKE A
BUDDHIST

HOW TO MEDITATE LIKE A BUDDHIST

CYNTHIA KANE

Hier phant publishing

Cover design by Emma Smith
Cover art by Steinar | Shutterstock

Hierophant Publishing
www.hierophantpublishing.com

Library of Congress Control Number: 2019957480
ISBN: 978-1-950253-00-5

Print book interior design by Frame25 Productions
Illustrations by Chathuri_suga

Stories at the opening of each chapter are taken from
either *101 Zen Stones* (Rider and Company, 1919), *Zen
Flesh and Zen Bones, A Collection of Zen and Pre-Zen Writings*
(Anchor 1961), or otherwise appear in the public domain.

For those wanting to live with ease.

By the practice of meditation, you will find that you are carrying within your heart a portable paradise.

—Paramahansa Yogananda

Contents

Introduction

Have you ever felt anxious, disconnected, or over-whelmed, like you're constantly running from one thing to the next? In the modern world, with so many activities and responsibilities, each completed task often opens up new obligations, leaving little time for anything else. For many, this persistent lack of silence, space, or personal time can lead to a life filled with stress, worry, or even resentment.

There are, of course, periods of stress in everyone's lives from time to time; but when stress becomes chronic and "normal," we can easily get to the place where it seems like life is running us rather than the other way around. The result can be a drain on our health and vitality, a lack of time and attention with the people we love the most (including ourselves!), and a cloud that hangs over our lives and obscures our perception of reality.

If you have felt any or all of this, let me start by telling you that I've been there, too. Years ago, my stress and anxiety were so bad they used to wake me up in the middle of the night, my mind racing with all the things I had to do each day and imagining the worst-case scenarios for all of them. Sometimes it felt like my tongue was swelling up in my mouth and I couldn't breathe. I thought something was wrong with me. After all, I had tried everything I could think of to "fix" what wasn't working in my life. I tried changing myself, my work, and my relationships; I moved cities and switched careers; I would adjust my schedule and lessen my responsibilities. But no matter what I changed, my sense of being overwhelmed stayed constant. It wasn't long before I concluded that there simply had to be something broken in me at a fundamental level. I became certain that I would never experience the kind of peace, presence, and purpose I so desperately craved and that I often saw in others.

Then, in February 2011, tragedy struck. Mauricio, my first love, died while kayaking down a river in Costa Rica, when he got caught in a swell. The moment I found out, I felt like my limbs were pinned to a surface. I couldn't move; I had no control over my body. The news left me exposed, broken open, and vulnerable. The pain was unbearable, and nothing I did seemed to make any difference. I could barely eat or sleep. Even when I could physically move again, I found there was no position, no activity, and no thought that could give me any relief. On the plane to Costa Rica with nothing to do but think, my mind swirled in a frenzy that seemed to call up every thought and emotion I had ever had. Like a hurricane picking up everything it touches and tossing it somewhere else, leaving destruction in its wake, I focused obsessively on death, life, love, meaning, work, fear, loss, and back to death again—a jumbled pile of thoughts I couldn't make sense of. I craved even a single moment of calm and wished that something—anything—could entice my crazy mind to take a break.

Mauricio's death had pushed my anxious thinking and fear to a new and now destructive level. My mind churned like a storm, despite all efforts to slow it down. In the days after his death, I tried distracting myself with music, movies, and computers, but all of this only seemed to make my anxiety worse. When I finally couldn't take it anymore, I started popping sleeping pills and drifted out of consciousness.

It wasn't long before those pills became more important to me than food. Even though I slept fourteen hours a day, I still felt exhausted during my waking hours. The hurricane in my mind continued and with it the thinking, wondering, and disbelief. My physical health began to deteriorate as well. Something had to change.

Maybe you believe, like I do, that some opportunity, a signal flag marking a new path, will often appear in your life when you need it most. Mine came in the form of a note from a friend a few weeks later, when she forwarded me an email about a writing and meditation workshop at the Shambhala Meditation Center of New York. I had never been to the place or even heard of it. But the idea of writing about my loss coupled with the meditation benefits they described felt like it might be a port in the storm for my hurricane mind.

That very first night at the Shambhala Center I began a meditation practice that, over time, would change my life. Today, I'm happy to report that I spend the vast majority of my days away from the path of the hurricane mind. I am calm, present, relaxed, joyful, and connected in a way I could only dream of before. And while I still have anxious and stressful moments, they are moments instead of days—and, most importantly, these feelings no longer paralyze or derail me. If you had told me eight years ago that I would find peace in my life, form deep connections with others, see beauty in the world, stop judging and evaluating myself constantly, and change my relationship to fear, death, stress, and anxiety, I would never have believed you. Yet, here I sit, writing this book to let you know that this is exactly what happened and that beginning a meditation practice was the cornerstone to this new way of life.

The impact on me was so profound that in no time I became a certified meditation and mindfulness instructor. And for those I work with, meditation has had similar benefits, helping ease their social anxiety, insomnia, and stress. I've seen meditation help people tap into their creativity, be more productive at work, and find overall well-being greater than they have ever felt before. I've seen marriages grow more intimate and loving and parents connect with their children and grow more peaceful within their families. I've seen people accomplish more with less effort, reduce their blood pressure, start sleeping better at night, and reset their relationship with food. Many say that they've started taking the worrisome thoughts that occur in their minds less seriously, which has created more joy, laughter, and adventure in their lives. Just imagine for a moment what any one of these benefits could mean for your life.

In addition to my own experience and that of my students, countless studies have measured the benefits of meditation on the body, mind, and spirit. In fact, it's difficult (if not impossible) to find a scientific study that hasn't concluded that meditation is good for you. A cursory internet search will deliver a variety of peer-reviewed studies showing physical, psychological, and spiritual results.

On a physical level, meditation can make you healthier:

- Regulates blood pressure
- Lowers heart rate
- Lowers cholesterol
- Normalizes blood sugar
- Increases fertility
- Reduces insomnia
- Decreases chronic pain
- Improves circulation
- Optimizes the immune system
- Increases the youth hormone DHEA

On a psychological level, meditation can change the brain:

- Alleviates depression
- Increases contentment

- Boosts self-confidence/self-esteem

- Reduces reactionary behavior

- Improves decision-making skills

- Enhances concentration

- Reduces test performance anxiety

- Reduces compulsive behavior

- Reduces ADHD and ADD symptoms

And finally, on a spiritual level, meditation can enrich your practice:

- Deepens sense of faith

- Increases feeling of connectedness with life

- Increases feeling of safety

- Increases intuition

In addition to all of the above, there are some key benefits to meditation from a Buddhist perspective. We will go deeper into these in the chapters that follow, but for now I'd like to start with the idea that meditation helps you to rediscover the quietness that lies inside you and provides access to an awareness and presence that is not affected by your past or the uncertainty of the future. Through meditation, you begin to connect with the inherent goodness within, or what Buddhism refers to as your Buddha-nature. While you may be accustomed to looking outside yourself for answers from others, Buddhism contains the radical idea that you already have the answers you seek and meditation is a tool by which you can access your own truth.

Buddhism also teaches that each of us has the power to relieve our own suffering. We are our own healers, and we have everything we need within ourselves. Suffering in this context refers to anxiety, discomfort, pain, embarrassment, shame, and/or self-loathing. Meditation is a way to change your relationship to this suffering, because it changes your relationship to your thoughts and your emotions. By practicing meditation you become a witness to whatever is happening, no longer attaching yourself to it or resisting it, but simply observing it. You are able to observe difficult thoughts and emotions and allow the sensations to be there, without letting them lead you. The more you observe and the less you judge, the more you heal.

Meditation invites you to find out who you are, and to be who you are exactly as you are, without judgment. In my experience, meditation can help restore what stress, anxiety, and being overwhelmed has taken from you, by bringing back peace, tranquility, and meaningful connection with others, as well as ease, energy, and joyful living. During meditation, we learn to be with ourselves in the best and worst of times. We accept ourselves as perfectly imperfect, dynamic, and ever-changing. This in turn allows us to see others in the same way, bringing a sense of compassion and connectedness into the world.

You may not believe that the practice I will teach you in the following pages can bring the same to you. But if you're willing to commit to it and stick with it, meditating like a Buddhist will change your life.

What to Expect from This Book

No religion or spiritual movement is more known for its association with meditation than Buddhism. While there are many schools of Buddhism, this book will teach you basic meditation practices and their benefits from a Buddhist perspective that would be applicable to most schools: relaxing, becoming aware of the present moment, and observing your thoughts. You do not need to be a Buddhist or want to become a Buddhist to practice meditation. Meditation does not discriminate—the benefits are for everyone.

This book will teach you what you need to know to start meditating right now, today. In fact, throughout these pages I will be asking you to set the book down and meditate with me. After all, you can read about this practice—and that's important so that you can be prepared and learn what to do—but the only way to really experience the benefits of meditation is by doing it. By the time you reach the end of this book, you will know what meditation is and isn't, the very simple tools you need to practice, the many types of meditations to choose from, some of the obstacles you will encounter when practicing, and how to incorporate meditation into your life with a meditative outlook. I've even added structured programs for a 10-Day Meditation Challenge, a 30-Day Meditation Challenge, and a 1-Day Home Meditation Retreat.

Each chapter begins with a Buddhist story or teaching and ends with one or more Explorations. These hands-on practices and journal prompts bring to life the concepts of Buddhist meditation and mindfulness in ways that are simple yet profound. You can try them out as you read and return to them again and again as you build your meditation practice.

Ever since I learned meditation, I've been eager to share what I know with others so that I can pass on the gifts that I found during one of the most difficult times in my life. I hope that this practice opens up new pathways to peace and joy in your life and the lives of those around you. To that end, this book aims to dive in and get you meditating right away. That's one of my favorite things about meditation—that it is so profoundly simple a child can do it, while also being so rich with possibility that you can spend a lifetime exploring it.

For now, take a deep breath in and out, and let's meditate . . .

The Gifts of Meditation
and Mindfulness

A horse suddenly came galloping down the road.
It seemed as though the man riding it had some-
where important to go. Another man, who was
standing alongside the road, shouted, "Where are
you going?" The man on the horse replied, "I don't
know! Ask the horse!"

Before I began practicing meditation, much of the time I felt as if external events were dragging me along to the next thing on my to-do list. The future was always coming fast and in a way I couldn't control no matter how hard I tried. I did not feel centered, grounded, or at peace. The result was that I spent much of my time feeling anxious, stressed out, and unhappy.

When I wasn't worrying about the future, my mind often lingered over my past, stuck in moments of regret or pain that brought on a sense of sadness. Vacillating between these two states kept me out of touch with the present moment, and as a result I reacted to almost every stimulus that came along, whether that was the words or actions of others or the thoughts that seemed to arise out of nowhere and that I believed without question.

Living like this often left me feeling overwhelmed, emotionally cluttered, and in a rush. I was going through life like a busy, senseless robot— unaware and mostly unhappy. The irony is that on the outside my life seemed pretty normal given the pace of society, but on the inside I was suffering, clinging to life even as it seemed to be spiraling out of my control.

On a physical level, all this worry also caused breakouts, weight gain, and stomach issues. There were times when my body would simply shut down for twenty-four hours, as if I had the flu, and I'd have to lay in bed and rest. I would occasionally wake up with red bumps all over my body, which I found out later were stress hives, and I developed sties in my eyes and would have to put warm compresses on them and sleep with a mask. While I thought these were isolated incidents at the time, I know now that they all came from stress and being overwhelmed.

Today, after incorporating regular meditation into my life, I'm happy to say that for the vast majority of time, I no longer live this way. Rather than staying stuck in the past or fearing the future, I'm here now, in the present moment. Compared to my old way of being, my anxiety is practically gone. All the physical symptoms of stress I was experiencing above have gone away. I respond to situations instead of reacting to them. I am clear about my goals and direction and rarely feel overwhelmed. Most shockingly, time seems to have opened up and slowed down, and it feels like there's more of it available as I know I can accomplish what I need to with ease and grace. I am charting my own course, choosing in each instant how I want to interact with the world and adjusting my own path.

Simply put, my life is much happier today, and there has been a direct correlation between establishing a regular meditation practice and lessening the suffering in my life. For those of you familiar with Buddhism, this will come as no surprise, because the primary goal of Buddhism is to address and deal with the suffering in our lives, and meditation is one of the most important practices it advocates to help do so.

When I say suffering in this context, I mean a mental state of things like worry, dissatisfaction, judgment, anger, anxiety, and the like. These are different from physical pain, which occurs in the body, such as when you break a bone or have a headache. Suffering is something that only occurs in the mind and, as I witnessed firsthand through meditation, is often a result of our thoughts.

The Three Poisons

Buddhism explains that mental suffering occurs from desire, aversion, and delusion, which together are called the three poisons in most Buddhist schools. Let's take a look at these, as they will be key things to watch for in your mind as you begin your meditation practice and we will refer to them throughout the book.

Desire

The first poison that causes suffering in the mind is the result of *desire* and attachment. In other words, think of what happens when you want something but you don't get it—the new car, a new house. The more attached you are to the thought, *I need this in my life to be happy,* the more you will agonize if you don't get what you want. Buddhism reminds us that in this life, no one gets everything they desire and if we are attached to what we desire then mental suffering is the result.

Aversion

The second poison is the opposite of desire and causes suffering when we have a mental state filled with dislike, *aversion*, or, in extreme cases, even hatred. For instance, we don't want certain things to happen and yet they come to us anyway. Perhaps we don't like particular people, yet they are in our lives in ways big or small. Anger, jealousy, and resentment are all states of mind associated with aversion, and they all cause mental suffering.

Delusion

The final poison is what Buddhism calls *delusion*, or ignorance. This is the most esoteric of the three poisons and therefore the hardest to write about, especially at an introductory level. But, in short, delusion refers to a mental state that cannot see the perfection in everything that happens. For instance, consider an event in your past when someone has not acted in a way you think they should, such as returning your affection or following your advice. When situations don't go as we planned, or fit our mental picture of what *should* happen, or when people disappoint us through their action or inaction, mental anguish and suffering are the result.

The Three Antidotes

Buddhism also offers us three mental states we can cultivate within ourselves that are antidotes to the three poisons, and these are the mindsets of generosity, loving-kindness, and wisdom. If our minds are focused on cravings or dislikes or delusion, we experience our day-to-day existence differently than if we are focused on generosity, loving-kindness, and wisdom. These are some of the mental states I was actually looking for when I walked into my first meditation session—although I didn't realize it nor could I have articulated it at that time.

Not surprisingly, Buddhism advocates that one of the best ways to plant and fertilize these wholesome antidotes in your mind is during your meditation practice, and we will be covering how to do this later in this book.

I also want to be clear that developing a meditation practice in my experience doesn't mean you won't suffer ever again. To be human is to feel sadness, anxiety, anger, and the like, but meditation allows you to see thoughts for what they are: feelings that arise, move through, and dissipate like dark clouds passing over a blue sky, rather than a hurricane-level force that consumes and controls you. Your thoughts and feelings will no longer fuel your actions. Through a meditation practice, you can begin to live in reality rather than in your thoughts about reality. Meditation helps us rein in the mind so we can take less seriously the incessant stories it spins.

Buddhism teaches that in order to lessen or eliminate that which causes us suffering (desire, aversion, and delusion), we cannot simply abandon, push away, or get rid of the thoughts and emotions. If it were that easy, everyone would do it. Rather, the first step is learning how to hold our suffering differently—how to breathe alongside it and change our relationship to it. When we gently view ourselves as we really are and life as it really is, we see that suffering is not something we need to dwell on, try to figure out, feel bad about, be embarrassed by, or be afraid of. Instead, we become witnesses to the fact that suffering is simply a part of life. By our acknowledging and relating differently to our suffering, it begins to lose its hold on us.

Meditation allows us to shift our intention and awareness from that which is causing suffering to that which reduces it. In this way we are training our minds, and the result is that outside of meditation we become conscious of where we are creating suffering in our own lives and the lives of others. The result is that we find ourselves speaking and acting in a way that is kind, compassionate, and fair to others as well as ourselves. Meditation is the glue that holds the mental states of calm and focus throughout the rest of our day.

While Buddhism teaches us how to approach the problem of suffering at its root causes, it also explains that each of us must make the journey within ourselves in order to eliminate it. Buddhism suggests that at the deepest level there is no problem, yet recognizes that we are suffering. Buddhism advocates meditation as a prescription for almost everyone, yet recognizes that no two individuals are the same. If you notice, you are getting your first taste of paradox. Buddhism, especially the Zen school, uses this as a teaching tool extensively because paradox is at the heart of our existence. Put another way, the world is perfectly imperfect, and it is through meditation that we can see the truth of this statement, in a way that the thinking mind can't fully comprehend. In my view, meditation can be seen as teaching the thinking mind to see beyond itself.

Meditation versus Mindfulness

So far, we've been discussing meditation. Now let's turn our attention to mindfulness. While meditation and mindfulness are interrelated, they are not the same thing. Each time I teach a beginners meditation class, I am usually asked the following questions: What exactly is mindfulness? What is the relationship of mindfulness to meditation? Let's begin by answering these.

The most straightforward definition of mindfulness is that it involves paying attention to the present moment with a nonjudgmental willingness to notice and be with *what is happening now,* instead of being consumed by the thoughts in your head. You can bring mindfulness to literally any part of your day: Pay attention to the way the toothbrush bristles feel when brushing your teeth rather than brushing quickly with your focus on finishing. Notice the sights and sounds around you as you drive rather than focusing on your destination and what you will do when you get there. Become aware of your emotions during a difficult conversation rather than ignoring them and thinking about what you will say next.

In fact, take a moment right now, wherever you are, and notice the sights, sounds, and smells around you. Try to do so without judging anything as good or bad or right or wrong. Just notice where you are. Notice how your body feels. Notice that you are breathing. Every human takes thousands of breaths each day, and many of us do so without noticing even one of them. Do so now. This is your present moment. You are practicing mindfulness.

These are all examples of being mindful of the external or physical world, which is a vital beginning and grounds us in the present moment. There is also the practice of being mindful of your thoughts. Notice when you have a thought of self-judgment, or self-rejection, and when thoughts of desire and aversion arise. Being mindful keeps you present and helps you appreciate the moment you're in rather than stressing and worrying about the one you're not in (past or future). A good friend of mine likes to say that "worry is like paying interest on a debt you don't owe." Another saying I like is that "99 percent of our worst days never happened, except in our own minds." When you bring more calm and space to your life via mindfulness, you give more energy to the life you're actually living than the one going on in your head.

Another aspect of mindfulness is to observe, rather than judge. This means no longer constantly judging things as good or bad—or, more accurately, noticing when you do. So many of our judgments are just mental habits. When you practice mindfulness, you become an observer, letting things and others be how and who they are. This often results in seeing situations with kind eyes, becoming more compassionate, and being open to the opinions and needs of others.

Through mindfulness, we can extend this compassion to ourselves. Part of the human condition for most of us includes that we have a deep-seated idea that we are "not enough," and this is evident in the multitude of advertisements we are bombarded with daily ("you must buy this or have that to be complete"). Furthermore, most of us have been our own worst enemy and harshest critic for as long as we can remember, often chastising ourselves internally with statements we would never say to anyone else. For instance, how often do you say things to yourself like, "That was so stupid of me," or "I'm such a loser." These statements cause suffering in our being, and being mindful of how you judge yourself is the first step to releasing these harmful thoughts.

One of the things I love most about mindfulness is that you can practice it at any time and in any place simply by bringing your attention to the present moment. In this way, a mindfulness practice is an immediate invitation to be here, now. Of course, it's natural that our minds will carry us off in thought and captivate our attention, as thinking is what the mind does best (just like the lungs breathe air and the heart pumps blood). When we notice our mind has wandered, we simply bring our attention back to the present moment and begin again.

Seen in this light, meditation is the formal practice of mindfulness. It comprises settling in and finding a bit of physical calm and then paying attention to whatever rises and falls in your experience: thoughts, emotions, physical sensations. You create a meditation practice by carving out time to sit and do this on a regular basis. Taken together, mindfulness and meditation help take you out of living in your mind and direct you back toward living in reality. The more you do this, the more you'll find that it's often the mind that is causing you to suffer, not reality itself.

Explorations

The following explorations are not meant to take the place of formal meditation practice. Rather, they will support your formal practice and help integrate what you learn and experience during meditation into your everyday life.

Mindful Moments

Mindful moments are different than formal meditation, but they will help you de-stress, rest, and feel more at ease in general, and you will quickly see how mindfulness can be practiced throughout your day. Below you'll find specific practices you can start to incorporate into your daily life.

Mindful Breathing

One of my students described a morning during which she had been rushing around from one thing to the next when she was suddenly struck by the overwhelming sensation that no matter how fast she went, she wouldn't have enough time. Instead of panicking, she leaned back in her chair, closed her eyes, and focused her attention on her breathing. After just thirty seconds, she felt like she could go back to what she had to do with a different mindset. Even if all you have is thirty seconds, pausing and paying attention to your breath can be just what you need to slow down, get present, and see things differently.

STOP

This exercise offers a more structured way to recenter yourself, and it can be done wherever you are. The acronym will help you remember the steps:

> **S**top whatever you're doing.
>
> **T**ake a deep breath and let it out.
>
> **O**bserve just one thing—it could be something in your environment, a thought, or a feeling.
>
> **P**roceed by returning to what you were doing or changing course.

This exercise is a simple version of a body/mind check-in and takes just a few moments to do. The acronym—for **C**hest, **A**rms, **L**egs, and **M**ind—makes the practice easy to remember. You can close your eyes or keep them open, silently moving your attention from place to place.

- Start by checking in with the physical sensations in your **chest**. Notice any pain, temperature, pressure, or vibrations.

- Do the same for your **arms**, moving from the shoulders down into the hands and fingers.

- Next, move your attention to your **legs**, really investigating what you feel.

- Finally, bring your focus to your **mind**. Breathe through whatever thoughts and emotions are happening for you right now.

30-Second Body Scan

Most of us work at a desk for hours a day, hunched over our keyboard, staring into a bright screen. Staying stationary for long periods of time can cause a lot of tension in the body. To help counteract that, whenever you get up to take a break, consider it a cue to do a quick 30-second body scan just to check in. To start, close your eyes and move your attention from the top of your head to your feet, noticing any places you feel tension. Breathe into them and then release the tension with your exhale. You can do this for every part of your body, top to bottom, or you can focus on whatever area is creating the most discomfort. (We'll discuss a longer version of a body scan later in this book, but many meditative moments can be accessed by shortening longer practices, which will help you restore a sense of calm to the present moment.)

Closing Your Eyes

Recently, my toddler came down with a double ear infection combined with an upper respiratory infection. At one point, he refused to take his medicine, and I could feel the frustration building inside of me. He needed this medicine, yet I knew the more I tried to force it the less willing he'd be. We were on a collision course.

So I closed my eyes. I sat on the floor with him standing next to me and just closed my eyes. This small act centered me, letting all of the stress of the moment go, and I was able to notice and distance myself from my intense attachment to giving him the medicine right then.

When I opened my eyes and felt differently toward the situation and he could see that I was more calm and centered, my son agreed to take the medicine. Just the simple act of closing your eyes in difficult moments has a tendency to make them easier to navigate.

Everyday Music

I use this practice when a certain sound is getting on my nerves or distracting me. To work with sound in a mindful way, close your eyes and focus on what you hear in your environment as your anchor. Become aware of the ones that are close to you, and ask yourself to listen to them as though they are your favorite music. Investigate the cadence, rhythm, tone, and volume of the sounds. Expand your listening to underlying sounds or steady background noise outside—traffic, faraway sirens, the wind moving through the trees. Even doing this for just a couple of minutes can reframe your current experience.

Kitchen Mindfulness

I designate certain regular activities in my life as mindfulness practices. So anytime I'm washing the dishes, I make it a habit to pay attention to the water on my hands, how the sponge feels on my fingers, the motion I make while cleaning. Anytime I get a paper towel, I consciously slow down. One of my favorite mindfulness practices that I use in the kitchen (and beyond) is counting, which always brings me back to the present moment. Sometimes I pause and count to ten and then come back to what I was doing. Or I count my inhales as I continue chopping or stirring (*Inhale one. Exhale. Inhale two. Exhale.*), up to ten.

Gratitude

I find that lunch is a good time to take a bit of a break during the day. Many of my students don't have time for lunch and so they eat at their desks. If this is you, never fear—you can still take a mini break. As you sit at your desk, instead of looking at social media or getting lost on the internet, why not take out a pad of paper or start a journal and write down three things you appreciate so far about the day, about you, or about your life? This simple practice has the power to shift you into a more relaxed state.

Meditation Journal

Based on my own experience with journaling and meditation, I'd encourage you to keep a meditation journal in which you'll write down your experiences as you begin and continue your meditation practice.

While the format is up to you, I suggest you keep track of time spent meditating, write down any changes you notice in yourself, and record some of your experiences as they come up. For some people, simply keeping track of the days they meditated revealed a correlation between meditation and how they felt the rest of the day. For many students, the days they meditated in the morning were the days they felt less stressful and more productive.

Let's begin our practice with a few moments of journaling now. Take a deep breath in and out, and spend some time writing in your journal about the following: Take a moment to think about the purpose you'd like a meditation practice to have in your life and why you want to start one. Some students are drawn to meditation to feel more calm, to have more energy, or to relieve anxiety and depression. Others come to meditation wanting to find a sense of peace and purpose and hope to build their capacity to tolerate difficulty or uncertainty. Understanding why you want to meditate is the key that will keep you coming back to the practice again and again.

Getting Started with Meditation

Nan-in, a Japanese master during the Meiji era (1868–1912), received a university professor who came to inquire about Zen.

Nan-in served tea. He poured his visitor's cup full, and then kept on pouring. The professor watched the overflow until he could no longer restrain himself. "It is overfull. No more will go in!"

"Like this cup," Nan-in said, "you are full of your own opinions and speculations. How can I show you Zen unless you first empty your cup?"

Before I actually learned how to meditate, the very thought of it seemed so complicated. In order to do it right, my anxious brain told me, I'd have to invest in special cushions, incense, gongs, and singing bowls. I couldn't possibly get anywhere by just sitting in any old place and breathing.

Yet this is the fascinating paradox of meditation. It can tame and calm the complexity and chaos of a harried mind with nothing more than two simple things that are available at all times: you and your breath. Even with all the different kinds of meditation and all the different options available in terms of posture, space, time (all of which we'll get to in this book), there are really only three steps that are absolutely required:

1. Preparing and showing up

2. Relaxing and choosing a point of focus

3. Paying attention

Let's take a closer look at what each of these requirements means.

Preparing and Showing Up

Maybe you're familiar with the Woody Allen quote that 80 percent of success is showing up. Well, when it comes to meditation, showing up is 100 percent of it. Cushions and incense don't mean much if you're not showing up to practice. And yet just showing up can present a real challenge. Our days are jam-packed. We have to take care of the kids, go to work, prepare and eat meals, clean the house, exercise, pay the bills, go to appointments, finish projects, keep up with friends and family, and more. At the end of any given day, we're often only capable of vegging out in front of a screen or going to bed. Time is often the biggest obstacle when it comes to meditation. It can often fall to the bottom of an endless to-do list and get pushed off to another day. Before long, it's been a month, and soon it's not a part of our lives at all.

As I teach my students the basics of meditation, I stress the importance of just showing up for the first thirty days, no matter what else may be going on in their lives, because it's usually within that time you'll begin to see and feel the benefits of the practice. (You'll find an outline of a 30-Day Meditation Challenge later in this book.) There's a Zen saying that goes, "You should sit in meditation for twenty minutes a day. Unless you're too busy, then you should sit for an hour." The most chaotic days when you feel you don't have time to meditate are likely the days you need it most.

While the basics of meditation are simple, there are a number of options in terms of space, meditation posture/position, and other considerations that will help you get ready to begin your practice. The following are some of the options available to you.

Make Space

While you don't need a special space designated for meditation, it can be helpful to establish a regular spot just for this purpose, especially when you're first starting out. This sets up sensory cues around that particular space that will become a signal to your body that "this is the space where I am safe, still, and can relax." Even after you are accustomed to meditation and no longer "need" the space, you may find you enjoy having an area set aside for it.

Your meditation space can be very simple, but it should be somewhere where you will not be disturbed. This is probably the most important aspect to choosing a meditation space. Your home office, the corner of a living room or bedroom, or even a large closet—if that's the only place you know you won't be disturbed—will be fine.

If you have the space to do so, you may wish to set up a small table with flowers or some object that signifies tranquility or peace for you. In Buddhist temples, you will almost always see a statue of the Buddha on an altar or table for exactly this purpose. While decorating or embellishing a space for meditation is by no means a requirement, doing so can be another cue to help you show up and relax.

Another preparation tip is to limit your potential distractions as much as possible. This means making sure your television, your phone, and any music are turned off and letting others in your house or work environment know that you're going to go meditate. You may also wish to hang a "Do Not Disturb" sign on your door. If you are interrupted, try not to allow the interruption to end your meditation practice, but instead settle back in once the interruption is over and meditate even for just a few minutes so that you end the session in a state of calm and relaxation if possible.

Take a Seat

Once you have designated a spot, there are several options for how to position your body for meditation. For now, let's focus on choosing a sitting position.

To begin, I recommend you either sit in a chair or on a cushion on the floor. No matter which you choose, you want to be comfortable, alert, and maintain good posture, all of which will ultimately help your practice. It's difficult to relax, focus, and pay attention if you're uncomfortable, and this will actually make it harder for you to show up regularly. The goal is to sit with a straight spine, but not so rigidly that it's uncomfortable. Imagine that your tailbone is reaching down toward the earth and your head is floating toward the sky. Tuck your chin slightly to release the back of your neck.

If you choose a cushion on the floor, I recommend sitting with your legs crossed, allowing your knees to relax downward to the earth. Sitting on a cushion keeps your hips higher than your knees, which is key to making this position comfortable while maintaining your alertness. Other options

include kneeling or sitting back on the cushion with your calves on either side.

There are round cushions designed for meditation called zafus, and they are often combined with a larger square cushion called a zabuton, which goes underneath.

Neither a zafu nor a zabuton is required for Buddhist meditation, but if you would like to experiment with these, there are numerous options for purchasing them online. In general, there are a number of mats, cushions, and pillows that can work for the

purpose of meditation, so feel free to explore your options to find the one that's right for you. Some people also find they are just as comfortable on the floor with no cushion.

For many people in the West, sitting in a chair is a practical alternative to floor positions. New students of mine sometimes think sitting on a cushion on the floor is necessary for Buddhist meditation, and I want to be clear that nothing could be further from the truth. Some of the best meditators I

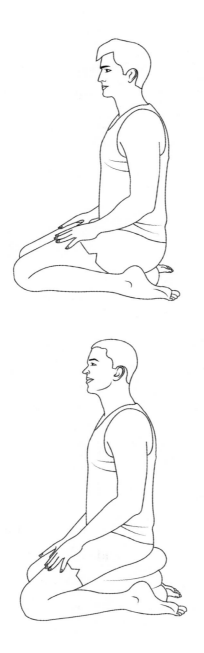

Getting Started with Meditation   31

know prefer a chair rather than a cushion. Sitting in a chair also takes pressure off your hips and knees, so if you have any range of motion issues or old injuries, a chair is the perfect choice.

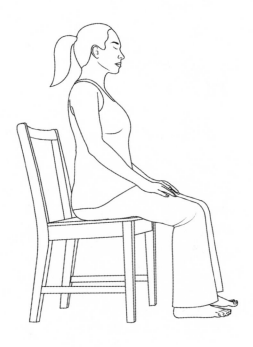

As with sitting on the floor, it's important to maintain good posture, and choosing the right chair is important here. Ideally, this would be a straight-backed chair or even a backless chair, which will encourage you to sit up straight. Your favorite comfy

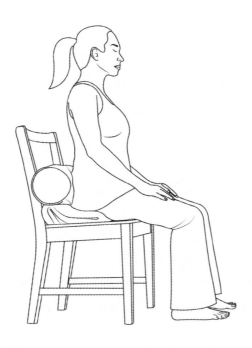

chair that you sit in to read or watch TV may be wonderful for those activities, but it's likely not the best option for meditation, as it may promote slouching or drowsiness. No matter which chair you choose, your back should be straight with your feet resting firmly on the ground.

Settle into a Posture

When people think about meditation, they often have images in their minds of men sitting with their hands in different positions or of spiritual iconography with special hand positions known as mudras. Special mudras are not required for meditation, and while they've been around since ancient times, they aren't often used in modern secular meditation practice. However, if you'd like to try meditating with a mudra, here are two simple ones to try.

Dhyani

Dhyani is used widely throughout many different meditation disciplines and is in fact known as the mudra of meditation. You may see images of the Buddha sitting with his hands positioned in his lap. In dhyani, the back of the right hand rests in the palm of the left hand, with the tips of the thumbs touching each other. This mudra symbolizes the triumph of enlightenment (the right hand) over the world of illusion (the left hand) and is said to encourage inner peace.

Gyan

Gyan is another popular mudra that you may see in a variety of images of people meditating in a seated

position with their legs crossed. Gyan consists of holding the thumb and forefinger together with the remaining three fingers straightened outward. It is said to encourage focus and wisdom.

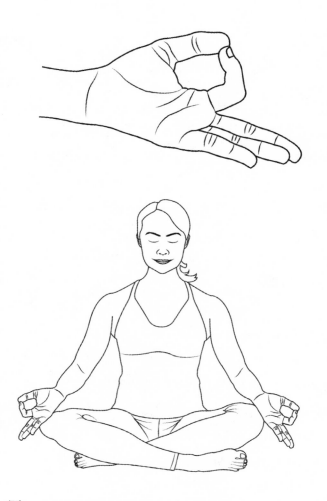

There are many other mudras that are associated with a number of different goals and benefits. However, be assured that simply resting the hands on the thighs works just as well.

Focus Your Gaze

Depending on what feels comfortable to you, I recommend closing your eyes or keeping them half-closed. If you choose half-closed, your gaze should be cast downward a few inches in front of you with a soft focus, not looking at any one thing in particular. The idea is that you limit any visual distractions. In the Zen tradition, adherents often sit facing a wall when meditating for exactly this purpose.

Set a Timer

Finally, I strongly recommend using a timer to start and stop your meditation. Whether you choose to meditate for five, ten, or twenty minutes (more about choosing a time in a moment), a timer actually helps your mind to relax and focus. You can set an alarm on your phone or download a meditation app, like Insight Timer, that has a timer. Using a timer reinforces your commitment to the practice, because once you've chosen a specific stop time, whether it's five minutes or twenty, it's important to continue to stay present and redirect your attention until the end. The timer encourages you to hold off any urges to get up and quit, so that you can stay curious about what happens moment to moment. You can open your eyes and look at the time if you need to, but then close your eyes again and come back to the practice just as you would after the mindful scratching of an itch.

These are the basic things you'll want to do to prepare prior to your first meditation session. I've also included some additional information in the Explorations section, which answer the common questions I get from students at the beginning of new meditation classes.

Relaxing and Choosing a Point of Focus

Once you are ready to begin, the next step is to sit down and allow the mind and body to become calm. You might not be feeling calm at first, and that's perfectly normal. Your mind may be racing and your heart beating fast, but it's integral to Buddhist meditation that you bring your physical body into stillness. There's an old saying I like: "If you bring the body, the mind will follow." I've found this particularly true for meditation. Just sitting down and relaxing the body, taking a few deep breaths, will calm the mind. The next step is to settle into this relaxation, and choosing a point of focus will help you do this. Let's explore what this means in a little more depth.

There are essentially two different "schools" of meditation when it comes to focus. The first school emphasizes a focal point, or "anchor," at the outset, and the meditator is instructed to concentrate on this point throughout the meditation. Examples of this kind of focal point include bringing your attention to your breath; naming the breath (thinking *inhale, exhale* as you breathe); repeating a short prayer, word, or mantra; or counting in your head from one to ten over and over again. The purpose of having a focal point is to give our restless minds something to do instead of rushing around from thought to thought like they normally do. This is not unlike giving an absorbing puzzle or teaching toy to a child; it fixes their attention and calms them down, while helping them train their minds to problem-solve. Eventually, much as a child learns to remain calm and control their reactions as they grow up and no longer need the puzzle or toy to do so, the mind also learns how to control its reactions to thought and emotion, and the focal point may naturally fade away in favor of silence or emptiness. With a focal point, the key is that anytime you notice that you have become distracted or lost in thought, you simply return to your anchor and begin again.

While you can turn anything into your point of focus, the most popular is the breath. As I mentioned in the last chapter about mindfulness, we are always breathing, yet most often we are unaware of it. Breath is the most constant and important aspect of life, so it naturally provides an accessible point of focus. You can refine the focus on breathing to wherever you feel your breath the most—in the rise and fall of your belly, the expansion of your chest, or the temperature and flow through your nose.

Go ahead and close your eyes and take a moment to notice your breath. Feel your inhale and exhale. This simple focus on the breath is all you need to be able to do in order to start meditating.

The second, more esoteric, method begins with a focus on the silence in between your thoughts. For this approach, you would settle into your space and your chosen posture/position, and then bring your attention to your inner silence, also described as inner stillness, emptiness, or awareness. Inevitably, especially in the beginning, this inner silence will be broken by random thoughts and feelings. Instead of attempting to otherwise occupy the mind with a repeated focal point, however, the meditator is instructed to welcome the thought and then let it go, so that they are neither ignoring it nor clinging to it.

Some teachers instruct students to say *Thank you* to their mind when they realize a thought chain has taken them away and then return to focus on the silence. Another popular tool for helping the mind return to presence with this method is that when you notice your mind getting caught up in a thought chain, simply remind it by saying inwardly, *We can think about that later; right now we're meditating.* This signals to the mind that you are not dismissing anything important—you are merely reinforcing that there is a time and a place for thinking and a time and a place for being silent. After this acknowledgment, you simply bring your attention back to the silence in the present moment.

Nearly all forms of meditation fall into one of these two methods, and neither is superior to the other; it really is a matter of personal preference. Both will result in you being in the present moment. In the beginning of your practice, spend a little time with each method to see which one works better for you. Most people find that they prefer one way over the other, and once you've determined which one you like, stick with it. Choosing one approach is preferable to switching back and forth, as it allows you to go deeper into the practice over time.

Paying Attention

Prior to that weekend at the Shambhala Center, I had never paid much attention to how I interacted with myself. I never realized that many of my thoughts about myself were hurtful, negative, and judgmental. During those first few meditation sessions, my thoughts went something like this:

I can't be doing this right. I have no clue what I'm doing. I should just stop. What's wrong with me? I can't do anything lately, I'm not even sure why I'm here. What was I thinking? I'm wasting my time, and the instructors' time, too. Your mind is wandering again . . . Can't you just focus on the breath? Get back to your breath, Cynthia!

In the midst of this chattering, I heard the teacher say, "There's no need to get upset with yourself for getting distracted or disturbed by your thoughts. Just say to yourself, 'thanks for sharing,' and refocus on your breath."

Thanks for sharing? I don't think I'd ever said anything like that to myself before. It occurred to me that I had never consciously just let myself *be*, without deciding I was good or bad, right or wrong, better than or less than. Paying attention and simply noticing my thoughts without judgment was completely foreign to me.

I find this to be true for my students starting out as well. For some reason, it doesn't feel natural to have thoughts and not take them seriously or to not get distracted by them. It's hard because our thinking, storytelling mind is programmed to evaluate everything, and it has a way of convincing us that everything it thinks is *soooo* important.

Allowing our thoughts to be without judgment, without giving them über-importance, can feel strange, even a little dangerous. There is no forcing, resisting, attaching, or wanting to fix them. This is what happens when you pay attention to your thoughts as if you are an uninvolved observer: you notice your thoughts, but you aren't consumed by them. This is where the internal mindfulness I spoke of in the previous chapter really comes into effect.

What has happened for me and so many of my students—and this is my hope for you too—is that meditation has changed my relationship to thoughts. They no longer become the absolute truth—and as a result, they no longer control you.

This brings us to one of the key insights of Buddhist meditation, and that is the realization that your thoughts, or that voice in your head, is not who you really are. Thoughts come and go, arise and fall away, but there is an awareness, or presence, behind the thoughts that watches them come and go.

For me, this was a major revelation. I had always taken my thoughts so seriously, because I thought the thoughts in my head were "me." Meditation is the place where you can experience yourself differently, as something greater than thought, perhaps for the first time in your life.

Meditation provides an enormous opportunity to distance yourself from some of the thought patterns, beliefs, and stories that contribute to your suffering. The worry, anxiety, regret, fear of failure, and all the other mental states that cause suffering are mostly the result of thoughts, and when you see that they aren't you, that they rise and fall on their own, you realize that you don't have to take them all so seriously, even if only for the period of time you are meditating, and your suffering lessens as a result.

The realization that *you are not your thoughts* is one of the gifts of meditation that Buddhism is perhaps most known for. This principle forms the basis for another fundamental tenet of Buddhism called anatta. This is the idea that the voice in our head is a type of illusionary "me" that we are all identified with and breaking this identification permanently is the key to ending suffering once and for all. A full discussion of this tenet is beyond the scope of this book, but suffice to say that in meditation we can experience the peace that exists beyond the thinking mind.

Of course, paying attention to what arises in your mind will offer other gifts of insight. For example, during meditation you may receive an inspired idea on the next step you should take in navigating a difficult situation, or you may gain clarity on your true feelings about something that prior to the meditation you had been unable to ascertain. You may also find peace and calm in a way that you had not before—although, remember, not feeling peaceful and calm during a meditation does not mean you have "failed"; be with what arises. Because we are all unique, the additional gifts of insight are as numerous as there are people who meditate.

These three steps—showing up, relaxing/focusing, and paying attention—are the basics of Buddhist meditation. If you are doing these, you are practicing. You now have everything you need to begin meditating, and by just learning about it and practicing the mindfulness exercises we discussed in the last chapter, you may already be experiencing some of the benefits of cultivating this kind of gentle attention in your life.

In the next chapter, we'll explore some of the different methods of meditation available that can help you explore and deepen your meditation practice. Before we do so, please take a look at the Explorations below, as I have included a cheat sheet for your first meditation and some other helpful information to remember as you get started.

Explorations

When I first started meditating, I wanted something very simple and to the point that I could follow to help get me begin my practice, and this is something my students have often asked me for as well, so I'm including my own personal cheat sheet for you. In this section I'm going to share with you a basic step-by-step outline of a session so you can start meditating right now. I'll also cover some additional points to keep in mind before you sit, as well as answer some common questions.

Your First Meditation Session

Do you remember the first time you backed a car out of a driveway? That process, for someone who's never done it before, is a chaotic swirl of input for the brain and body. You feel your feet on the pedals and your hands on the wheel; you're getting visual input from the mirrors as well as your own eyes and audio input from inside and outside the car. You have to gauge distance, speed, and the intent of others on the road. If you're a regular driver now, you can likely do all this without too much trouble, but when you first tried, your brain hadn't yet made a habit of any of these highly coordinated skills, attention, action, and reaction.

In a sense, the same is true when learning meditation. Getting quiet and tuning in can reveal an overwhelming amount of chatter in the brain and activity in the body, and you don't yet have any experience to rely on. Remember, your practice is about beginning again. So when you get caught up in the thought of "I'm doing this wrong," you want to say to yourself, *Thanks for sharing,* and come back to your point of focus. By coming back to your point of focus, you know that you're doing the practice, and that means you're doing it right.

With this in mind, I have put together a short list of what the actual process of meditation looks like. Think of this as a little cheat sheet to get you started, and once you've meditated a few times, you won't need this list anymore.

1. Take your seat.

2. Settle into the space.

3. Close your eyes or focus your gaze down in front of you.

4. Take one or two deep, calming breaths.

5. Start your timer.

6. Choose your point of focus.

7. Whenever you notice you're distracted and caught up in a thought or a story, just observe it, perhaps say to yourself, *Thanks for sharing,* and come back to your point of focus.

8. Continue the above for the set time period.

When you're inside the meditation, remember that it's normal that your thoughts will take you on all sorts of detours. This is where the *practice* part of meditation comes in. After all, what are we working on when we meditate? We are working on the process of paying attention and refocusing when our attention wanders.

Here's an example of what your distractions during meditation might look like:

- Thinking, *I'm bored . . . This is stupid . . . I should be responding to emails right now.*

- Shifting in your seat before you remember to move mindfully.

- Getting upset about not moving mindfully.

- Feeling silly for getting upset about not moving mindfully.

- Thinking, *Feeling upset is an emotion, and emotions are temporary.*

- Coming back to the present moment and the anchor of your breath, feeling it pass through your nostrils.

- Wanting to get up.

- Recentering on the breath again.

And so on . . .

The point is, no matter how many times you want to get up and stop, or get distracted, or are overtaken by a powerful emotion or story, you refocus on the present moment. *Refocusing and beginning again is the practice.* You can always begin again.

Here are a few other helpful, gentle notes to bear in mind as you begin your practice.

There's Nothing to Accomplish

The point of meditation is not to become the best meditator. In fact, accomplishing anything is beside the point. Approaching meditation as something to achieve or accomplish will lead to judging, evaluating, and comparing ourselves and our experiences to others'. Instead, we want to allow ourselves to exist in the present moment. In this practice, we want to do less and be more; to try less and notice more. In this way, we experience presence.

Lotus Position Not Required

When it comes to meditation postures, the first image that probably comes to mind is what's commonly called lotus position. Lotus position involves crossing your legs so that both feet are off the floor and resting on each opposing thigh. This opens up the hips, keeps the spine straight, and reportedly assists with keeping the mind awake and focused. However, it's a challenging position for many—especially for those with compromised knees—and you may already be wondering how on earth you're supposed to sit like that for any length of time. Well, while lotus position has its benefits, you are absolutely not required to sit this way in order to meditate. If you like the position, and you find it helps you show up, relax, and pay attention, definitely continue to sit this way. But rest assured that there are plenty of other options when it comes to posture in meditation.

You're Doing It Right

Before you start meditating, it's important to know that you may feel like you're doing it wrong. But I want to stress that the only way to do it wrong is if you're not doing it at all. I've had students who've said, "Well, I spent the whole time thinking and I didn't focus on my breath." Or, "I had a hard time staying awake—I kept falling asleep." Or, "This time I didn't feel calm at all. I felt more anxious, like I wanted to crawl out of my own skin."

Each of these students was doing the practice.

Meditation offers us an infinite range of experiences, and no session is going to be the same as the next. One day, you might easily pay attention to your breath for ten minutes, and then the next you might find yourself unable to concentrate at all. You might finish a session and feel energized, with a rosier outlook on people and situations, or you might feel rushed, agitated, annoyed, or gloomy. Acknowledge this before you start meditating, so that you can allow yourself to be as you are during meditation, without judging, evaluating, or curating your experience.

Physical Comfort

If you have an itch, feel free to scratch it, and if you're uncomfortable, feel free to adjust your seat. However, any movement should be made mindfully—that is, with gentle awareness before and during the shift—and then bring your awareness back to your anchor afterward. For example, I find that after fifteen minutes, my left leg often falls asleep, so I move my attention from my breath to my leg as I move it. It's an odd sensation, feeling the blood rushing back to my foot as I shift it. The movement becomes a part of my meditation. Once the sensation dissipates, I place my attention back on my breath.

Sitting Alone versus Sitting Together

Some people prefer to sit alone in meditation, while others thrive on the energy of meditating with a group. I do think at different times in your practice you'll prefer one over the other. Some people find it can be easier to stay in meditation when they are sitting with others. One isn't necessarily better than the other, nor has either been scientifically proven to be more beneficial than the other. As with many things when it comes to meditation, experiment with both, and whichever is your preference is the way to go. Depending on where you live, a quick search for "meditation near me" may provide a variety of Buddhist and secular options for group meditation.

When to Meditate

The final consideration in establishing your meditation ritual is, of course, time. In the beginning, I recommend trying to meditate at the same time every day. You can add meditation to your existing habits by meditating in the morning after you wake up, go to the bathroom, wash your face, and brush your teeth. Another good time is around the midday slump, around 3:30 or 4 p.m., when it feels like you need to get another cup of coffee and maybe a sweet snack to make it through the rest of the day. Instead, try sitting for ten minutes and you'll feel just as refreshed and likely with more energy. I had one student who set her phone to go off every day at 4 p.m. for meditation and teatime. Another would set an alarm to go off around noon, at which point she would find a room at work to go sit in. Before long, even when she wasn't by her phone, her coworkers would let her know, "Your phone went off. It's meditation time!" Schedule it, and integrate it into your existing routine.

Common Experiences During Meditation

Any experience you have during meditation is normal; however, some of my students like to know ahead of time what experiences they may have during meditation so they won't be as scary or anxiety-provoking when they happen. Most of these common experiences are related to the release of stress from your body.

- *Seeing colors*: Some students will start to see colors during meditation, often in splotches, swirls, or flashes. It could be greens, violets, blues—really, any color can show up—or sometimes it can just be black.

- *Twitching*: As our bodies start to relax, our muscles can start to twitch.

- *Swallowing excessively*: I have a tendency to start swallowing a lot more than normal during meditation, as my throat relaxes and saliva flows more freely.

- *Experiencing body aches and pains*: When we get quieter, we might notice uncomfortable sensations in the body that we had been suppressing, especially pain. Adjusting your posture may help with this.

- *Falling asleep*: It's very common for beginning meditators to feel drowsy at first, and it may mean that you need to get more rest at night. If this happens to you, make sure you aren't meditating lying down.

- *Losing track of time*: When meditating, you may lose your normal sense of time and space—or experience a "gap" in time. It can feel like a session was only one minute long instead of ten or twenty.

- *Feeling strong emotions*: As with pain, submerged emotions can sometimes rise into our consciousness while meditating. This can be alarming, but it's totally normal.

- *Crying and laughing*: With or without emotions, crying and laughing are natural physical reactions when the body releases stress.

Again, any experience you have is normal. If any of these experiences become overwhelming at any time, open your eyes and then close them again and return to your point of focus.

Deepening Your Practice

Daiju visited the master Baso in China. Baso asked: "What do you seek?"

"Enlightenment," replied Daiju.

"You have your own treasure house. Why do you search outside?" Baso asked.

Daiju inquired: "Where is my treasure house?"

Baso answered: "What you are asking is your treasure house."

Daiju was enlightened! Ever after he urged his friends: "Open your own treasure house and use those treasures."

The first meditation practice I learned that weekend at the Shambhala Center was samatha (sometimes spelled *shamatha*). One of the most fundamental of Buddhist meditation practices, samatha is essentially a calming meditation that encourages you to concentrate on the breath and to return to that each time you notice that your thoughts have carried your mind someplace else.

Samatha meditation is closely connected to what is likely the most well-known of Buddhist meditations, vipassana. Often translated as "insight meditation," vipassana implies that in meditation we have the ability to *see things as they really are*, or to observe and understand the nature of our reality. One of the reasons they are closely connected is that practicing samatha (relaxing and choosing a point of focus) is what leads to vipassana (insight).

As you may have noticed by now, the meditation we covered in the previous chapter is a combination of both samatha (calming) and vipassana (insight) meditation techniques. It invites you to samatha in relaxing and choosing a point of focus and then to vipassana as you pay attention to what arises in your consciousness. It's important to point out that the deepest level of vipassana referenced by Buddhist masters typically takes years of meditation to reach.

At the same time, this is all relative, because many people have reported receiving powerful insights after meditating for just a little while. As I have already mentioned, the impact on my own life from meditation has been profound, and this is certainly a result in part of increased insight, or vipassana.

After that first weekend at the Shambhala Center, I continued to practice the meditation I was taught that weekend for quite a while before finding out there were other forms I could try. In my own case, samatha worked for me, in that my daily practice was consistent and uncomplicated. Even as I learned about other meditation techniques and experimented with them, samatha was the practice I kept coming back to, the one I did the most.

While I believe the meditation technique we covered in the previous chapter is an excellent place to start, everyone is different, so I also believe it's good to try different types of meditations or at least be aware of them, because you may find you like some of them better, or you may find that in combination with other techniques, they help you deepen your awareness even further. To that aim, this chapter will be devoted to explaining some other types of Buddhist meditation so you can experiment with these as well.

If you remember from chapter 1, the three poisons in Buddhism are desire, aversion, and delusion. These are the roots of our suffering as human beings. Note that these are all inner states; they come from within our minds. Buddhism offers us three antidotes—generosity, loving-kindness, and wisdom—and the following meditations are designed to help you cultivate these qualities in yourself, therefore reducing suffering in the process.

Generosity

Desire and attachment are perhaps the best known of the three poisons, likely because our modern world takes desire to a whole new level. We are bombarded daily with advertisements and other images that emphasize that we need to buy this, look this way, or experience that, otherwise we won't be complete. Fueling the idea that we need more is the concept of scarcity, or the belief that there isn't enough love, happiness, or money for everyone. This sense of scarcity and want extends not only to material possessions, but also to emotions, relationships, and ways of being. Because we live in a society that promotes that we are not enough and that we never have enough, the seeds of human suffering around desire are planted in almost every aspect of our lives. We are rarely still, or satisfied, or whole or at peace, because we are constantly told we are not *enough as we are.*

One of the things I love about Buddhism is that its teachings run directly counter to society's messages and the concept of scarcity. Buddhism maintains that we are in fact whole already and there is nothing we need to add to ourselves to be complete. This is why meditation, which relies on what is already inside you, is the prescription Buddhism offers for what ails us. A world in which every moment is complete unto itself is a world of peace and true contentment, out of which our natural response to the needs of others is to be generous.

Generosity Meditation

When we meditate on our own wholeness and contentment, it naturally leads to a feeling of expansive generosity.

As you begin your meditation, recite these phrases silently to yourself:

I am enough.

I have all I need.

I am whole.

I am content.

Consider as you go through your daily life what it would look like if you always felt as though you had everything you need, and in fact you have so much, you don't ever need to worry about not having enough in the future. How would this change your relationships with those close to you? With your coworkers? Your community? The world?

Gratitude Meditation

Closely related to generosity is gratitude. In fact, one could say that gratitude, much like a feeling of wholeness, is what can lead you to generosity. Gratitude could also be viewed as the opposite of desire, because when we are focused on being grateful for what we have, the unquenchable thirst of desire ceases or is at least lessened.

In this meditation, as you sit, you bring your attention to all that you have to appreciate in your life right now. Start small. You can think of your body, the ground beneath you, and how the earth is supporting you at this very moment. You can widen your awareness to the places you live and work, the sense of safety you feel, your friends and family, nature and the trees that give you oxygen to breathe. When you notice that your thoughts carry you away to something else, simply bring your attention back to gratitude.

Meditation that celebrates gratitude can be a very powerful practice. In addition to taking your focus off desire, it provides relief from some states of mind that are also under the umbrella of suffering: feeling disconnected from others, lonely, unworthy, like you've failed, or like something is wrong with you or your current situation. These are all excellent times to practice gratitude meditation. A multitude of studies show that focusing on what we appreciate helps our overall health and well-being and builds a sense of warmth and connection with others.

Generosity is felt when we know we are whole, content, and grateful for what we have, and adding this meditation to your practice can help you experience this.

Loving-Kindness

Metta is a Pali word that is typically translated as "loving-kindness," although it's also translated as the single word "love." You may have heard or seen this term before, as it's one of the Buddhist terms that has made its way into Western popular culture. Metta has a deeper meaning than the type of love we hear about in love songs or see in romance movies, though. Loving-kindness is more akin to an attitude of detached goodwill that we want to cultivate toward everyone in our lives, including ourselves. In this way, metta is the antidote to aversion.

Metta Meditation

I mentioned before that it was during meditation that I first became aware of how much of my internal self-talk consisted of judging and berating myself. Through meditation, I noticed how I was often my own worst critic and regularly spoke to myself in ways I would never speak to others. If you too suffer a lot of negative self-talk, metta meditation can help you extend loving-kindness to yourself and change the way you speak to yourself in the process.

Metta meditation is particularly helpful when you're dealing with other people that you find you have a dislike or aversion toward or when resentments toward others are clouding your mind. Remember that with resentment, you are the one who suffers, which is why resentment is sometimes described as "ingesting poison and waiting for someone else to die." Many of my students have said that adding a metta meditation to their practice has had a profound, transformative effect on their relationships at home and at work. By extending others the spirit of loving-kindness during meditation, we often find that the way we interact with them outside of meditating changes for the better as well. How and why this actually works are not always explainable, but I have had students come to me on more than one occasion and state that after practicing metta meditation toward someone they were having difficulty with, the other person "miraculously" changed, and at other times students have said that extending love and kindness to the other person in meditation allowed them to better understand the other's point of view, thus reducing conflict.

When we extend metta to people we don't like, we can see how it is different from most traditional ideas about love, which is almost always focused on those special people in our lives, such as family members, significant others, and close friends. These special people have a place in our metta meditation too, as they provide an excellent example of where positive regard and goodwill are easy for you to find within and extend outward—that's why it's recommended that we begin our metta meditation with them in mind.

While there are different ways to do metta meditation, the method I will teach you involves five parts, and they all begin with the same basics we covered in the previous chapter. Once you have taken a seat either on a chair or cushion and calmed the body and mind for a few moments, turn your attention to the metta aspect of the practice.

First, think of some of those special people in your life you love and hold dear—parents, children, close friends, even pets. Choose one in particular and imagine yourself sending loving-kindness their way. You want for them to experience nothing but goodness in their lives. Some people say a little internal mantra or prayer as they extend metta in their minds, like this one:

May you know joy.

May you know peace.

May you be free from suffering.

May you live with ease.

The exact words are not important; the goal is to cultivate the feeling of loving-kindness within yourself, extending those feelings outwardly toward this person in your mind.

The second part of metta meditation is to think of someone whom you are neutral toward. This could be someone you see every day at the bus stop, someone you walk by, or perhaps the girl behind the counter at your local bakery. In this part of the practice, you endeavor to extend the same loving-kindness you felt in part one to this person that you hardly know. Recite your mantra again to yourself:

May you know joy.

May you know peace.

May you be free from suffering.

May you live with ease.

Most people can do the first two parts with little trouble, but it's in part three where things get uncomfortable. For this step, think of someone you're having difficulty with, someone you feel resentment toward, and do your best to extend them the same measure of loving-kindness. I don't recommend starting with a traumatic relationship or with someone who sparks too much of an emotional response. You'll want to ease into this at first, but extend loving-kindness to this person you currently do not like, offering the same words:

May you know joy.

May you know peace.

May you be free from suffering.

May you live with ease.

While part three is the most difficult for many people, you may find that you have more trouble with this next part. You've likely guessed it by now, but I want you to extend loving-kindness to yourself. Try to bring that same goodwill you have toward those you love to yourself.

May I know joy.

May I know peace.

May I be free from suffering.

May I live with ease.

For the final part, I want you to expand your focus to the whole world. Here is where you are imagining that you have given up aversion to anyone or anything. I like to pretend that I am flying high like a bird, looking down from above and extending goodness to all beings in all directions:

May you know joy.

May you know peace.

May you be free from suffering.

May you live with ease.

You can do one meditation and offer these phrases to everyone mentioned, or you can spend one session simply focused on sending out loving-kindness to yourself or to someone else. For instance, when you're feeling down on yourself, isolated, or misunderstood, I encourage you to turn to the portion of metta meditation that focuses on sending loving-kindness to yourself. You'll want to welcome all the sensations you feel, and if you don't feel anything during the meditation, that's okay too.

Tonglen Meditation

Another form of meditation that can be used to counter the poison of aversion is tonglen. Tonglen is not a loving-kindness meditation per se, but rather a meditation that *transforms* feelings of anger, fear, hurt, and sadness. It helps us relax into our own pain and be present for the pain of others. This practice is different from others in that it asks that you breathe in the suffering, negativity, and pain of others and then breathe out calmness, clarity, and joy. You may think it's odd to breathe in suffering and breathe out calm; before I encountered tonglen, I was only aware of small grounding meditations where I was taught to inhale love and joy and breathe out anything that was no longer helping me. However, from a Buddhist perspective, breathing out anger and pain is a way you send toxins into the universe, which isn't a kind or helpful thing to do, as it promotes more suffering.

To try tonglen for yourself, settle into your meditation space and take a few deep, centering breaths. On your next inhale, imagine that you are breathing in your own suffering. Your anger, pain, anxiety, sadness, and hurt are being gathered up into your breath and into your body, where they are transformed. On your next exhale, send that transformed suffering out on the breath as loving-kindness and compassion for yourself. Imagine this new, beautiful energy filling the space around you and infusing the air.

If you find this difficult, it might be easier to start with breathing in the suffering of someone you know and care about, and then on the out breath sending love, support, and compassion to them. You can do this for yourself and someone with whom you may be arguing or struggling, by breathing in your frustration and theirs and then breathing out clarity and forgiveness for them and for you. You can even do this meditation for all people, feeling the pain of all people and then on the out breath sending love and calming energy to all people who are hurting or in conflict.

Wisdom

This final category of the antidotes brings us into deeper philosophical territory. As I mentioned earlier, Buddhism teaches that what we think of as the "self" is more akin to a collection of ever-changing thoughts, sensations, and stories swirling around in our conscious mind.

The mind is a consummate storytelling machine. Events happen in our lives, and the mind makes up a story to go along with it. Sometimes these stories are harmless, but at other times they can be a source of suffering. It's in these moments when we say that stories are also the source of delusion and wisdom is the antidote.

Here is an example of the power of story. Let's say you have a good friend you haven't seen in a while, and the last couple of times you planned to meet, your friend has called to say she couldn't make it. The storytelling part of your mind may start to think, *Maybe she doesn't want to see me. What if she's angry with me for some reason?* You recall a minor argument you had with her a few months ago, and you wonder if that's the reason she's canceling your plans. You replay the argument over in your mind, reliving your own irritation and frustration, and you become increasingly hurt that your friend would refuse to see you over something like that and even resent that she's avoiding you. Before long, you are caught in a loop of anxiety, anger, and hurt feelings (suffering). When your friend finally calls, she apologizes and explains that she's had a terrible month and begins to confide in you all the things that she's been dealing with. It becomes immediately clear that she was never avoiding you, and you realize how your storytelling mind manufactured all of that suffering based on the simple fact that your friend canceled your plans.

This is just a small example of the million ways our storytelling mind habitually creates narratives to events in the world and highlights that these narratives are frequently wrong and a source of our suffering. It's important to notice here that the stories you told yourself were the root of your suffering, not the circumstances themselves. Wisdom is not getting the story "right"; wisdom is seeing the story *as a story.*

Another benefit of meditation in general is that you may find yourself better able to notice when the stories in your mind are causing suffering in your life. The next time you find yourself worrying about the future or in deep regret of the past, ask yourself, *Is there a story that my mind is spinning that is contributing to my suffering?* Simply noticing the story as a story is a step out of delusion and into wisdom.

Emptiness Meditation

His Holiness the Dalai Lama, the spiritual leader of Tibetan Buddhism, says that emptiness is the true nature of things and events. There is also a selection from the Heart Sutra of Mahayana Buddhism, some of the most quoted of all Buddhist literature, which is often pointed to in a discussion of wisdom:

Form is emptiness, emptiness is form
Emptiness is not separate from form
Form is not separate from emptiness
Whatever is form is emptiness
Whatever is emptiness is form

As you can see, Buddhism makes a connection between emptiness and wisdom. But what can this possibly mean? This question may be difficult to answer with the thinking mind, but meditation could provide us access to an understanding that is beyond thought or cultivate wisdom within ourselves.

To begin an emptiness meditation, once you are seated, contemplate the relationship between form and emptiness that is suggested by the Heart Sutra. Ask yourself, *What does it mean that form is emptiness and emptiness is form?* Rather than answer the question intellectually, sit with the question and see what arises.

An emptiness meditation can help us see the transitory nature of existence. The world is changing all the time, and incorporating an emptiness meditation into our practice may mean we see ourselves and others with less judgment and without labels, fears, or expectations. Everything that exists, for as long or as short as it exists, is a miracle, because it has all arisen from emptiness. This is a perspective of wisdom.

Meditating on the three antidotes is a great way to deepen your practice. Your practice may also shift at different times in your life, and this is completely natural. In my own case, after losing my first love I spent a lot of time doing metta (loving-kindness) and gratitude meditations. While pregnant, I did a lot of body relaxation and visualizations for a smooth and easy labor and delivery. Later, I did walking meditations on my way home from dropping off my son at day care. The more you get in touch with what you need, which comes from your regular practice, the more you'll know which meditation methods will help you. One way to choose what is best for you right now is to think about what may need gentle attention the most in your life at the moment.

Explorations

There are, of course, many kinds of meditation out there, and you may find over time that you are drawn toward particular methods. Some people absolutely love saying silent mantras, for example, while other people find it distracting. I've included a variety of techniques here (not all of which are necessarily Buddhist forms of meditation) that you may want to experiment with. Remember that there are no rules here; the point is to find out what works best for you.

Silent or Voiced Mantras

A mantra is a sound, word, or phrase that is repeated over and over. It can be repeated aloud, chanted, or thought to yourself silently. The word or phrase often isn't as important as the sound itself. *Mantra* means "vehicle of the mind," and like other points of focus we discussed in chapter 2, a mantra is often used as an anchor to keep the mind on track. There are religious mantras, and some people also use Sanskrit syllables, words, or sounds. Common syllables are *om, hum,* and *sah.* You can even use everyday words such as *love, peace,* or *joy.* You may want to choose one and say it over and over during your meditation.

Visualization

Imagine you have cut a fat, juicy lemon into pieces; now, in your mind, put a piece of that lemon in your mouth. Chances are just imagining this will make you start to salivate, even though there is no actual lemon present! This is a common reaction to this exercise and shows us that our minds are extremely powerful. Things don't have to be physically present for us to experience them in our minds.

Visualization meditations are guided imagery—they can help you establish a place in your mind where you feel safe; they can help you with physical pain, such as labor and delivery; they can help you with difficult conversations; and they can help you shift your anxiety and fear into feeling empowered. Think it and the body believes it; the key here is to make your visualization as detailed and sensory as possible, just as in the lemon example.

Body Scan

A body scan is another practice that can be integrated into meditation or done on its own to ease pain or help you get to sleep. Many people start their meditation by taking a few deep breaths and then move on to a body scan from head to toe. If you're experiencing tension, stress, or physical pain in your body, insomnia, or a physical imbalance of any kind, the body scan will give you deeper access to your sensory experience—how your body is right now, in this moment.

To begin, sit with your eyes closed and turn your attention toward your body, starting with the weight of your body and its contact with the chair or the cushion. Notice your feet on the floor. Then focus one by one on different parts of your body, starting with your head and scanning down toward your feet: head, forehead, face, neck, shoulders, arms, hands, chest, back, stomach, hips, legs, toes. For each area, say to yourself, *Relax* or *Soften* so that you can bring as much ease as possible to that part before moving on. During this practice, sensations within the body may get stronger. Your challenge is to breathe alongside these sensations, not push them away or try to fix them. Allow each sensation to be there and invite yourself to soften and allow what is.

Walking Meditation

Walking meditation is also known as *kinhin* in Zen Buddhism, and originates from Buddhist tradition. You can do a walking meditation anytime and anywhere. To begin, pay attention to your senses, feeling the ground beneath your feet, the movement of your arms and legs, the change in balance going from one leg to the next, the movement of your hips, walking slowly or quickly. Notice the feeling of your clothes on your skin, the cool air on your face, the sound of cars or birds. Observe and relax as you let your walking be natural and easy. When you find yourself distracted, bring your attention back to your next step. At the end, stop and experience what it's like to be standing. Notice the stillness. With a deep breath, bring the walking meditation to an end.

Standing Meditation

Standing meditation can be a good option for those who have arthritis or injuries or who experience discomfort when sitting. It can also keep you awake if you experience extreme drowsiness during seated meditation. For this meditation, stand with your knees slightly bent and your feet shoulder width apart. Your weight should be over the balls of your feet. Allow your arms to hang loosely by your sides. Relax your body and place your attention on your breath. Keep your shoulders where they are as you breathe naturally. Once you feel stable, close your eyes. Here you can keep your attention on your breath, count your breaths, notice any bodily sensations, or use a mantra—whichever practice feels right to you. If you find it difficult to have your eyes closed while standing, you can keep your eyes slightly open with your gaze cast downward a few inches in front of you.

I know from experience, and from teaching meditation to my students, that any of these practices can have a profound effect on your mindset, well-being, outlook, and mental and physical health. I find it to be an exciting and powerful paradox that these benefits come about through an action that has no specific goals. We don't sit on the cushion or on a chair with the intention of changing our lives, and yet that's exactly what happens.

Journal Prompts

Maybe at the beginning of this book you were intimidated by the idea of meditation. I hope you now see how simple it is to begin and that anyone and everyone can do it. By now you've learned the basics of meditation and how to explore your practice even further through focused meditation with the three antidotes. You may have already settled into a regular routine that you would like to work with for the time being, or you may still be exploring different kinds of meditation to find the right fit for you. It's also possible, however, that as you've started to meditate, you've noticed patterns that seem to be standing in the way of your ability to maintain or deepen your practice. Buddhism calls some of these patterns the five hindrances, and we'll explore these in more detail, as well as how to overcome them, in the next chapter.

In the meantime, however, keep checking in with yourself as you go and writing in your meditation journal so that you notice the changes in your needs and in your own thoughts and patterns as you learn to be more and more present to and accepting of what is. The following are some journal prompts that may help you along your journey:

1. How is your meditation journey going so far? Are you running into any obstacles? Are you seeing any benefits?

2. Which meditation techniques intrigue you? Try them out, and then journal about your experiences.

3. Think back over the past week. Can you see any times when your storytelling mind may have caused you any unnecessary suffering? How might your practice help you in future similar situations?

4. Make a loving-kindness list of all the people you can send loving-kindness to in metta meditation. You might be surprised how long the list can be!

5. Make it a habit to list five things you are grateful for each day. If it's difficult to think of things you are grateful for, consider things that you might not focus

on on a daily basis but are working for and with you all the time, such as your breath, your heart, or the earth beneath you. Did you receive a smile from someone today? Did you remember to take a deep breath when you were stressed? Even the smallest things are worthy of gratitude.

The Five Hindrances to Meditation
(And What to Do about Them)

*A Zen student came to Bankei and complained:
"Master, I have an ungovernable temper. How can
I cure it?"*

*"You have something very strange," replied
Bankei. "Let me see what you have."*

*"Just now I cannot show it to you," replied the
other.*

"When can you show it to me?" asked Bankei.

"It arises unexpectedly," replied the student.

*"Then," concluded Bankei, "it must not be
your own true nature. If it were, you could show it
to me at any time. When you were born, you did
not have it, and your parents did not give it to you.
Think that over."*

I left the Shambhala Center that first weekend floating on air and wrote in my journal that I was ready to commit to meditating every day. I had already felt the benefits of sitting for a single weekend, and I was hooked. I felt my energy soaring with a bright sense of possibility, and I thought that since I knew the practice now, continuing it would be relatively easy. What I didn't know then, but would soon find out, is that certain tendencies within me would try to slow my practice or even shut it down entirely.

I hadn't yet experienced what Buddhism calls the five hindrances.

One could say that if meditation is a way to calm an anxious, chaotic mind, then the five hindrances are the ways in which the mind fights back. These hindrances represent five common obstacles that, if you aren't aware of them, can derail your practice before it gets established.

For me, as well as for almost every single person I've taught, these obstacles have appeared in some form or another. They can lead you to think that your meditation practice isn't working, or that you're doing it wrong, or even that you aren't cut out for practicing. Once you know what the five hindrances are and you learn to spot and work through or even with them, you'll be able to keep your practice on track. Just like the Zen story reminds us above, these hindrances are not part of our essential nature.

The Five Hindrances

1. Desire

2. Aversion

3. Sloth and Torpor (Boredom and Sleepiness)

4. Restlessness

5. Doubt

You may notice that the first two hindrances, desire and aversion, are two of the three poisons we've examined already. That's because the three poisons—desire, aversion, and delusion—are so integral to our suffering that they will follow us into meditation and disrupt our practice. However, by learning to recognize these poisons and the others as hindrances, we become better equipped to work with and through them not only in meditation, but also in our daily lives.

Let's examine each of these hindrances in detail, as well as some ways you can overcome them.

Desire

We've talked a lot about how desire constitutes one of the core roots of our suffering and about how meditation can help us notice when our attachment to material possessions, people, social status, and the like become unhealthy and cause suffering. Now, let's examine how desire can manifest during our meditation sessions, or even before the session begins, sometimes preventing us from meditating at all.

One of the primary ways the chaotic mind uses desire to disrupt your practice is in the form of a thought, either before or during your meditation practice, suggesting that you should be doing something else—something that you really want to do instead. While the generosity and gratitude meditations we covered in the prior chapter will be helpful here, desire as a hindrance often emerges as some kind of physical distraction, subtle or acute.

For example, let's say you plan to meditate in the evening, but that afternoon you have the thought, *Well, I had planned on meditating tonight, but I would really like to go to dinner and a movie with my significant other instead.* To support this idea, your mind may come up with all sorts of reasons why this would be better than meditation: *We haven't seen each other much this week, and I really need to spend some time with him/her. It's important for our relationship.* This is a subtle way your mind can throw you off track and disrupt your practice. An acute example of a desire-based distraction that may arise during a meditation session may be as simple as, *I'm getting hungry. I should eat something and meditate another time.*

These simple examples illustrate how clever an anxious mind can be. There are, after all, perfectly good reasons to spend time with your significant other, and we all need to eat. What makes desire a cunning adversary is that whatever you are considering doing instead of meditation often feels right and good, at least in the short term.

When distractions like these occur, simply noticing them and being a witness to the energy they invoke within you can be enough to keep you on course much of the time. In other instances, when the desire is strong, it may take all the willpower you have to keep your commitment to meditate that day. This is one instance when discipline can be important to maintaining your practice. Over time this will get easier, and remember that very few are successful 100 percent of the time, so if you do opt for dinner and a movie instead of meditating one evening, remember to not let this become a reason to beat yourself up and stop meditating altogether.

Aversion

Aversion is another favorite tool the mind uses to throw our practice off track. Dislike, anger, and fear are all ways in which aversion can manifest and slow down or derail your practice. Let's look at dislike and anger first, as they are the most common forms of aversion.

Dislike often expresses itself as physical discomfort, and like other hindrances, it can manifest in subtle ways that may not be obvious as first. Some examples of how the mind may employ dislike to discourage you from practicing may come in the form of thoughts like these:

It's too cold in here to meditate (or too hot).

I can't meditate on this cushion—it isn't very comfortable.

My arm is sore. I'll meditate when it feels better.

These examples show how we may push an experience away from us out of what in reality may be simply mild discomfort. In this way, aversion is the opposite of desire. When you hear yourself make some sort of internal complaint about why now is not a good time to meditate, or that encourages you to stop meditating if you've already started, let that be your cue to check the hindrance of aversion and see whether the concern is real or if it's more of a mental complaint. For example, can you adjust the temperature or your body position to be more comfortable? And if you can't, are the circumstances you are dealing with really that bad? I have a good friend who cautions against waiting for or needing the "perfect circumstances" to meditate—if we do, we could be waiting for a long, long time.

Another tool of aversion is anger, which if it arises can make it difficult to show up and relax, one of the first steps to meditation. Anger can also occur in a subtler form; perhaps a thought pops into our mind which says, *I'm in a bad mood from an argument at work today. I don't feel like meditating right now.* Anger in its acute form, such as rage, can really knock us off-balance and make it hard to relax, focus, and observe. The irony is that it's in these bouts with anger that we often need meditation the most.

In these instances, I recommend starting your meditation session by extending metta (see chapter 3) toward yourself. Just like with resentment, when we are angry at some person or situation, we are often the one who suffers, as these negative emotions can only be felt inside of us. After you've extended loving-kindness toward yourself, see if you can extend it to the person or situation that has caused the anger to arise. Like we've discussed, sometimes just bringing nonjudgmental awareness to your feelings is enough to help them subside.

In addition to dislike and anger, fear can also come up during our practice and can prove to be a significant distraction. I once had a student who told me that in the beginning states of her practice she could only sit for five minutes at a time. After settling in, she would experience sudden, uncontrollable surges of fear. Why was this happening? In her case, there were some situations in her life that were the source of this fear, and meditation served as the first time she'd allowed herself to sit and become quiet long enough for the feelings to arise. Your body whispers warnings that only you can hear, so listen up! Meditation quiets the background noise and amplifies our inner voice. All healing is informed by listening.

I've found this to be true for myself and others as well, especially when first starting out. We spend much of our day pushing away feelings we don't like because they're uncomfortable and inconvenient. We don't want to feel sadness, grief, or anger (which is almost always a mask for fear), so we avoid it; we eat something, take in a movie, exercise, call a friend—or we engage in less healthy distractions, such as binge-watching TV, surfing the internet and social media, and turning to addictive, numbing substances like alcohol. We try to distract ourselves from our emotions rather than face them and find their source.

When you first start to sit in meditation, however, you will quickly realize that there is no place to run away from these strong emotions. Anxieties that we would normally try to dull may rise to the surface, and we have nowhere to go and nothing to do but to feel them.

This can be very unsettling, and the temptation, of course, is to quit meditating in order to avoid this. We may feel discouraged and blame the practice itself for making us feel bad, while becoming convinced that this isn't what meditation is supposed to be like. Our fear of facing these emotions can trick us into telling ourselves that meditation isn't working or is even making everything worse.

My student, for example, didn't think that these feelings of fear were supposed to be a part of meditation, so she would stop. Wasn't she supposed to be calm and peaceful and feel completely at ease? I smiled, because many of us have this same expectation when we first start meditating, but the truth is that sometimes we will experience the complete opposite, especially in the beginning.

So how can we work through this challenge? First, while it can be really difficult to do so, it's critical to remember that *any experience you have in meditation is the right experience.* It goes against what we've been taught and the stories we tell ourselves, but the first step to moving through this hindrance is to name and acknowledge that this, too, is part of your practice and it's normal to have these feelings.

There are a couple of other things to try when you find yourself facing fear or some other unpleasant emotions during a meditation session. The first is to simply locate the *sensation* of the emotion in your body and then put your gentle, friendly, and nonjudgmental attention there. For example, if you are in meditation and suddenly feel an upwelling of fear, ask yourself, *Where do I physically feel the fear?* Maybe it's a knot in the pit of your stomach or a fluttery feeling in your chest. Try to breathe alongside the emotion and pay attention to the sensation in your body rather than the story around it.

In my own case, shortly after I began my practice, I would experience bouts of anxiety during meditation. Following the advice of my teacher, I gave the sensations in my body all of my attention, and I noticed how they kept leaping away from my focus on it. The heat, the rapid heartbeat, the sensation of fear and claustrophobia, all of them raced from place to place. Instead of panicking, however, I was able to observe the sensations moving around with curiosity. Before long, I realized that all the physical sensations of anxiety were gone and I was able to go back to my point of focus, my breath, and complete the meditation session.

It is completely normal for strong emotions to arise in meditation, and you will want to push them away. But when we deny them, they can last longer. You may want to get up after five minutes and call it quits, but I invite you to do the opposite: sit alongside your discomfort and let it just be. Often, you will find that these emotions and the discomfort they cause will pass in a minute or two.

One final thing to consider is that the feelings that are coming up in meditation may point to other areas or situations in your life that need to be examined, sometimes with the help of a professional counselor or therapist. It's important to remember that meditation isn't a cure-all, but rather a helpful tool for your overall well-being. With this in mind, these experiences in your practice can help in showing you, through strong emotions, what other areas of your life need attention outside of your practice.

Sloth and Torpor (Boredom and Sleepiness)

Sloth and torpor are not frequently used in today's English language. They describe a state of laziness, apathy, or sluggishness that can arise and become an obstruction to your practice. This hindrance is often described as boredom or sleepiness, and I have found it more helpful to use these descriptors.

"Every time I meditate, I fall asleep," a new student complained. "No matter what, my head starts nodding and the falling motion startles me awake. Maybe I just can't do this." Experiencing acute sleepiness during meditation can be another way your mind tries to resist. I've had students tell me, especially when they tend to get sleepy or doze off after just beginning to practice, that they think they are simply not "cut out" for meditation.

The first step is to examine your sleeping habits and see if there are any changes you can make that will leave you more rested and refreshed in general. If you are getting an adequate amount of sleep at night, then it's likely that the sleepiness you're encountering is a manifestation of this hindrance rather than a physical need.

My next suggestion would be to check your posture. Are you keeping your spine straight? Are you sitting up with your shoulders back? If you do so to the point that it requires you to use your core muscles a little more than normal, you're less likely to fall asleep.

Another suggestion would be to go deeper into the sensations of your breath. Feel the air flowing in your nostrils, throat, lungs, and belly. Notice the temperature of the air you are breathing. You can repeat to yourself silently on the inhale, *breathing in,* and on the exhale, *breathing out.* If nothing else is working, try switching to a walking or standing meditation, which will certainly help keep you awake.

Lastly, it's important to always remember that no matter how many times you doze off, you can always begin again. You *are* cut out for meditation, so be sure to keep sitting for your set amount of time no matter how sleepy you may feel. Don't beat yourself up for falling asleep. Observe it, acknowledge it for what it is, and then start your meditation again.

Now let's look at boredom, as I have found with my students that this aspect of the third hindrance is the one more likely to apply. Why might that be the case? For starters, many of us have a cultural belief that we must be busy every waking moment of our lives with some kind of task. We may even have a history of self-judgment, also handed to us by culture, that if we aren't doing "something," we are lazy. Because of this, we've attached an enormous amount of self-worth to the idea of "accomplishment," even tying it to our own self-acceptance. Consequently, it can be very uncomfortable to let time go by simply sitting quietly in a room alone. Surely we can't just sit here, *breathing,* when there's so much to do!

Consider this: What if you are actually experiencing serenity instead of boredom? Remember, because meditation is at its core a practice of simply allowing ourselves to *be,* without expectation or occupation, many of us, especially when we are just beginning, feel a kind of mental pressure to do something more "productive," so serenity and peace are actually quite uncomfortable. *Nothing's happening!* the mind might scream. Believe it or not, this experience is more common than you may think.

If boredom is still a problem, then another approach I recommend is to focus your meditation on the sensations of boredom in your body and find ways to sit with them. You may discover after some time that, just like with sensations of strong emotions, your boredom will fade. You may also consider spending small amounts of time during your day "actively" doing nothing in addition to your daily meditation practice. Perhaps in the morning, instead of catching up on the news on TV or your phone, you simply sit in a chair and look at the scenery outside your window for a few minutes. The idea is to signal to your mind that it's perfectly okay to spend time devoid of accomplishment, and you may find yourself less agitated by the simple being of meditation.

Restlessness

Restlessness is common in Western culture. Just as strong emotions can waylay the practice for some people, others aren't able to sit because they feel they need to fix their hair, scratch their leg, get up and get another cushion, reposition themselves, and so on. This sense of restlessness stems from sources that are similar to those we explored regarding boredom. We spend most of our days in a constant state of doing. We wake up with a list of to-dos, we go through our day adding to that list and checking things off, and at night we mentally plan our list for the next day. Doing is how we exist, and meditation is something very different: *Nope, it's not time for that. Just sit.* It's hard to let go of the urgency we feel in our day-to-day lives so that we can sit quietly, observing and noticing the sensations of our breath.

If you're feeling restless when trying to meditate, first ask yourself a few simple lifestyle questions: Are you meditating right after you've had your third cup of coffee? Is there a better time of day for your meditation when you might feel more relaxed? Are you trying to squeeze in your meditation right before having to leave for another appointment? Restlessness can be solely a product of the mind in an effort to take you away from your practice, but it never hurts to spend a few minutes to see if there's a practical solution that may help.

Just as we learn to mitigate feelings of desire or attachment, it requires discipline to sit with restlessness until the feeling dissipates. As I suggested in dealing with the other hindrances, try to bring your attention to any part of your body that is associated with this feeling of restlessness. Do you feel it in your arms, legs, or chest? Simply observing the physical area in which restlessness manifests will often lessen it.

Lastly, and this goes with all hindrances, try to welcome the restlessness as a personal challenge. When you notice yourself wanting to pay attention to anything else, or get up and move positions, or give in to another hindrance such as desire or aversion, you've uncovered another choice point. This realization means that you're becoming more aware of yourself and your mind's tendencies and you have a choice in the moment if you give in to them or not.

Doubt

The final hindrance, doubt, is one of the mind's favorite tools to curtail or eliminate your practice. Unlike other hindrances that may be experienced in the body (desire, for example), doubt arises completely within the domain of the mind. In this way, it is similar to the poison of delusion.

You can experience doubt during meditation, but it will often manifest at other times of the day, tempting you to stop your practice altogether. For instance, you might doubt if you're doing it right, if what you're doing is really helping, or if you're wasting your time. You might wonder why you even thought you could do this, and you might decide this whole thing just isn't for you. The self-talk of doubt promotes suffering, elevates fear and worry, and keeps you in a state of suffering. Doubt might be telling you, "I'm not getting anything from this," when in fact the doubt itself is a tool of the mind and yet another way it tries to keep you from taming it.

There's another reason why doubt can be so potent. As human beings, we crave knowledge and certainty. But while we are able to assert some measure of control over ourselves and our environment, it's simply not possible for us to control everything or know everything, and meditation is a place where we can practice giving up our need to know and control things, if only for the period of time that we are sitting. These needs are so inherent to the makeup of the mind that it's no wonder it fights back and questions the validity of meditation.

When you notice doubt creeping in, the first step is to acknowledge it as a hindrance and name it silently to yourself as such: *This is my mind talking to keep me from practicing.* Then, take a moment to visualize yourself putting doubt on a shelf so that you can return to your point of focus. Relinquishing control and embracing uncertainty are big projects, but meditation is a wonderful tool to help you release the need for absolute control and embrace the natural, unpredictable flow of life. Doing so will, of course, be a factor in decreasing your personal suffering; when we embrace ambiguity in the world around us, we become more relaxed, more able to appreciate each moment for what it truly is, and our lives become expansive and free.

You may find that these hindrances are related or overlap one another in your own experience. That's not uncommon, as they all have the same source and goal; each is ultimately your mind's way of distracting you from relaxing into the present moment and being instead of thinking. Because each hindrance is a variation on distraction, the mindful cultivation of awareness and acceptance will help you in overcoming any hindrance no matter how it may be manifesting in your practice.

One of my teachers says, "When in doubt, practice." The most important thing we can do is practice. So keep it going, make it yours, and remember that the moment you get discouraged is the moment I invite you to come back. As long as you come back to your cushion, to your practice, you're doing it correctly.

Most people who meditate will contend with these five hindrances throughout their practice. Whenever they come up, simply acknowledge their presence without judgment, allow the experience to be as it is, and sit with the discomfort. This *is* the practice. You might even appreciate these hindrances as blessings within your practice, because they're waking you up, offering you a choice point, and showing you it's time to come back to the present moment.

I hope you've started practicing already with some of the formal meditation methods in this book. In the next chapter I'm going to give you three structured ways to get started: a 10-Day Meditation Challenge, a 30-Day Meditation Challenge, and a 1-Day Home Meditation Retreat. Try all three as you begin to meditate like a Buddhist.

Explorations

Sometimes it's difficult to remember what to do when obstacles present themselves in meditation, so in this section I want to share with you an acronym that may help the next time you encounter one of the five hindrances in your practice.

RAIN

One helpful method for dealing with hindrances that has been taught by the Insight Meditation school and author Tara Brach is called RAIN, an acronym for the four steps of the process:

Recognize what is happening.

Allow life to be just as it is.

Investigate with kindness.

Non-identification

In order to look at RAIN more closely, let's say for example that you are feeling restless and agitated during your session; you can't seem to focus, you keep thinking of things you didn't finish, and you keep wanting to leap up and do things (*I forgot to turn off the kitchen light, and I should do that before I meditate. Wait, these magazines are a mess, I'll just straighten them. I can't seem to get comfortable, maybe I need a new cushion . . . I'll just look for new cushions online really quick before I continue . . .*). You take a deep breath, and realize that you are encountering restlessness, one of the five hindrances. This is the first step of RAIN:

recognition. And this first step is arguably the most important. Because you are now familiar with the five hindrances, it will be easier to notice them when they crop up.

To continue with our example, now that you know you are restless, you can acknowledge to yourself that this is happening. You are naming and uncovering the problem. You might even say out loud, "I'm feeling very restless." There's no need to find a reason for your restlessness at this point or begin to build strategies to fight it; simply allow it to be.

The third step is to investigate. You may not always need to do this; for some, just recognizing and naming the issue will be enough to cause it to subside, but sometimes it can be helpful to dig a little deeper and see if you can find the root cause of your restlessness by asking yourself questions about why you think this might be happening. You can also investigate by locating the physical sensation of your issue in your body and focusing on that, as I recommended in the section above on anger.

The final step then is non-identification. This is a critical step. Instead of getting caught up in the idea of *being a restless person*—and any stories you attach to it, such as blaming yourself for being "unable" to sit still—permit yourself to see your restlessness as a temporary situation, one that will pass. You may be restless now, but restlessness is not part of your essential nature. Observe it, be curious about it, but don't let it become part of your identity.

Meditation Challenges:
10 Days, 30 Days, 1 Day

Once, a small boy was walking by the sea when he noticed an old man along the shore. The boy watched with interest as the old man crouched down, picked up a slim piece of driftwood, and drew a perfect circle in the sand with one graceful stroke.

"Grandfather," cried the boy, "How did you learn to draw such a perfect circle?"

The old man smiled. "I just tried, and then I tried again . . . here, why don't you try?" And he handed the piece of driftwood to the boy and walked away.

The boy began to draw circles in the sand. The first was too oblong, the second was too crooked . . .

but as time went by the boy's circles began to look better and better, until one day he crouched down, picked up his piece of driftwood, and drew a perfect circle in the sand with one graceful stroke.

It was then he heard a voice behind him, saying, "Grandfather, how did you learn to draw such a perfect circle?"

When it comes to meditation, creative pursuits, exercise, or anything that takes a regular commitment of time and energy, we might have all the information we need and be clear about our desires and intentions, but we still may not know where to begin. For me, that first step is often the hardest, and once I take it, I find myself wondering why it felt so difficult. To that end, I've gathered these three different challenges that will help you jump-start your practice. It's as simple as sitting down and setting that timer.

10-Day Meditation Challenge

This first challenge is a great place to start. Ten days is a relatively short period of time, but it's definitely long enough for you to start to appreciate the benefits of regular meditation and encourage you to make it a part of your daily routine. The challenge below also includes specific intentions to meditate with each day to help your mind focus and deepen your awareness.

Before You Begin

If you haven't already, establish your space as outlined in chapter 2. You might want to spend some time reviewing that section to make sure you have everything prepared (space, cushion, timer) to help you with the all-important task of showing up for this 10-day challenge. If you have a friend or relative you feel would be a great support for you during this time, consider inviting them to join you so that you can help each other stay with the process.

You'll also want to make sure you have your meditation journal handy and schedule some additional time before and after your meditation for writing. Each day, begin your journal entry by marking the date, and then make space for these three entries for each session:

1. Before you meditate: How are you feeling in your mind and body? What are your surroundings like today? What's on your mind, or what experiences are you thinking about?

2. Immediately after you meditate: What did you experience during meditation?

3. Before you end your session: In what ways you feel differently, the same, or neutral?

The Challenge

Each day of this jump-start challenge will consist of a 10- to 15-minute meditation practice. The intention for each day will be different, but the core meditation practice will be the same, and I suggest you do it at the same time each day for ten days in a row. If you miss a scheduled meditation session, simply begin again by returning to the practice when you remember to do so that same day or the next day. Here's an overview of what each meditation session will look like:

First, set your timer for ten or fifteen minutes.

Sit with a straight and relaxed spine. You want your back to be straight, but not so rigid that it's uncomfortable. Imagine your tailbone reaching down toward the earth and your head reaching toward the sky, floating atop the natural curves of your spine. Tuck your chin in slightly to release the back of your neck.

Begin by turning your attention to your breathing: each inhale followed by an exhale in an unending cycle. Notice the cooler air in your nostrils on the inhale and the warmer air on the exhale. You might also feel the breath moving your belly or expanding your lungs.

When you feel ready, bring up the day's intention word in your mind (see the list below). Use the word as your anchor, or point of focus, for the meditation. As distractions come up, you will continually return to this word.

As you think about the intention word, open yourself to the possibility of seeing images and feeling any emotions that help you connect with the meaning of that word. If and when you do experience images or have sensations in the body, feel free to let the intention word go in that moment and rest in the sensation within the body.

If you find you are telling a story or making a judgment related to this word, gently remind yourself to come back to the breath and the intention word itself and begin again.

Finally, take a moment to let go of any particular focus on sensations, the intention word, or the breath and just sit in stillness.

Come out of meditation by taking long, slow, deep breaths and slowly opening your eyes.

Intentions

Day One: Dedication

This first day, begin by reflecting on why you want to start this practice of meditation and what is going to bring you to your cushion each day. What's drawing you to sit with yourself?

Day Two: Generosity

What would today look like if you chose to be generous toward yourself and others? How can you express generosity throughout the day, whether through actions or words? Ask yourself, *How can I practice generosity today?* Use this as your mantra to come back to when you notice you're distracted, rushing, or somewhere other than the present moment.

Day Three: Discipline

Today is about recommitment. This can mean recommitting to the present moment, to being mindful, to your meditation practice, or all of the above. It means beginning again, starting over—this could be an assignment, a relationship, a dream. What are you going to recommit to today?

Day Four: Patience

Look for places today where you can soften and slow down. What would today look like if you expected everyone and everything to take its time? How can you bring more patience into your interactions with yourself and others today?

Day Five: Joy

Look for opportunities to be in flow today. Make choices that are going to help you feel healthy, successful, fulfilled, and joyful.

Day Six: Inquiring Mind

Challenge yourself to see clearly today, to let go of the story and focus on the direct experience. See yourself as fluid, constantly changing. There's no need to judge or evaluate yourself, no need to force or fix. See if you can simply allow yourself to be as you are.

Day Seven: Compassion

Today, commit to seeing yourself and others with friendly eyes. See the suffering in others as well as yourself, and notice that we are all the same. Offer compassion to yourself, strangers, those you know, and those with whom you're having a hard time.

Day Eight: Balance

Look for ways to find some middle ground today. Set aside exaggerations, assumptions, and thoughts of better-than and less-than and replace them by meeting people and scenarios just as they are.

Day Nine: Spaciousness

Where can you bring more spaciousness into your day? What areas need more room to breathe and bloom? What's no longer helpful that you can release to make room for what is?

Day Ten: Celebration

Today is a day for celebration. *You did it!* You've just spent the last ten days meditating, you did it for more than five minutes, and you have successfully worked to incorporate it into your daily routine. Reflect on the last ten days and honor your practice, celebrating each day and each session.

Once you've completed this 10-day challenge, take some time to write in your meditation journal about the experience as a whole. How did it go? Was it comfortable, easy, difficult? What did you learn? What surprised you?

30-Day Meditation Challenge

To cultivate the benefits of any practice, you have to commit to taking daily action. When you are ready, my hope is that you will expand your meditation practice with this 30-day challenge. You may have already started to see the benefits in regular practice by committing yourself to the 10-day challenge, and the 30-day challenge is designed to help you really see how meditation can improve your life in so many ways. I've organized it so that you can do six days a week for five weeks, though you may certainly do it every day. I have no doubt that you will see, feel, and experience the benefits after completing this challenge. The difference you'll feel with yourself, your relationships, and your environment will be all the proof you need to continue incorporating the practice into your day-to-day in small or big ways.

The Challenge

Similar to the 10-day challenge, you will be meditating for ten to fifteen minutes, preferably at the same time each day. Every week will focus on a different meditation, and you'll want to make time for journaling and reflections daily as well. Just as you did in the 10-day challenge, you'll prepare your space and begin and end each session with a journal entry. You'll follow the same meditation steps as well. See pages 116–18 from the 10-day challenge.

Intentions

For this challenge, you will focus on daily intentions that will work to help you cultivate a specific quality for an entire week.

Week 1: Observation

During the first week, you'll be doing mindfulness meditation, using any of the following concepts as an anchor. You can repeat it silently as a mantra, or just bring it to mind at the beginning and end of your practice.

- Curiosity

- Perspective

- Stillness

- Emotions

- Sensations

- Spatial awareness

In your journal, write about anything that surprised you this week or that you hadn't noticed before. It could be something inside you or outside.

Also reflect on any ways that observation showed up in your daily life.

Week 2: Courage

This week you will incorporate meditation on compassion, with a focus on how compassion can help you navigate challenges and stay present. This can take the form of metta (loving-kindness) or tonglen (breathe in suffering, breathe out love). We discussed these meditations in chapter 3. Alternatively, you can focus on one of the following intention words during your daily session:

- Self-compassion

- Love

- Fortitude

- Boundaries

- Honesty

- Loving-kindness

In your journal, write about any differences you notice from the beginning of the week to the end in terms of being able to stay present during difficulties, either while meditating or in your daily life. Was this hard for you? Easy?

Week 3: Discipline

In your third week, you may be starting to wrestle with some form of the five hindrances:

- Desire

- Aversion

- Sleepiness or boredom

- Restlessness

- Doubt

Use your time on the cushion to really sit with each of these ideas, uncovering new ways they are manifesting in your mind and body. Remind yourself that you can always begin again, and you can coexist alongside any of these hindrances and they will pass.

In your journal, reflect on any new ways you discovered to approach the discipline of your meditation practice. Celebrate the achievement of coming this far in your 30-day challenge.

Week 4: Flexibility

This week, you'll be focusing on softening and allowing whatever is happening for you during meditation. Use the following concepts as you meditate this week:

- Expansion

- Gentleness

- Warmth

- Resilience

- Adaptability

- Letting go

In your journal, write about any challenges or discoveries this week. Did these concepts make you feel vulnerable or empowered? How did you nurture yourself this week? How did your body feel?

Week 5: Right Action

In your final week, you'll reexamine what action, or doing, means from a mindful state. So much of meditation practice is to unlearn our very modern habits of staying busy and understanding our value as what we can accomplish, rather than what we are. Meditate on any of the following ideas:

- Mindful action

- Focus

- Doing one thing at a time

- Slowing down

- Flow

- Joy

In your journal, share any discoveries you made about how you can bring mindfulness into your actions. Then, take some time to freewrite about the whole 30-day experience: were there any challenges or celebrations, and what you feel you'd like to take into the next phase of your meditation practice, whatever that may be.

1-Day Home Meditation Retreat

If you've completed the 10-day challenge and the 30-day challenge, you have most likely also begun to build up your regular practice and may be ready to challenge yourself to a whole day of meditation.

This might sound intense at first, but spending a considerable amount of time in meditation during the course of a single day can bring even more calmness and deep insights. During this retreat, you will be alternating between sitting and walking meditation, practicing mindfulness during mealtimes, and observing what Buddhists call *noble silence.*

If you're already practicing with others or have been sharing your meditation journey, this 1-day retreat is a great opportunity to practice together. Having other people around you who are sharing a common experience and can help keep each other grounded in the practice can be immensely helpful. Of course, you can also do this retreat by yourself.

Set a Start Date

First, you'll want to decide when your in-home meditation retreat is going to begin and put it on your calendar. Let those you live with, or those you're in touch with daily, know your plans so they aren't alarmed if you don't answer your phone for the day.

While this is an all-day retreat, your actual retreat time will be between 9 a.m. and 5 p.m.

Set Up Your Space

In addition to your regular meditation space that you've prepared and set aside for your practice (see chapter 2), you may want to spend some time making sure the rest of your living space is inviting and clean, as you want to create as simple, refreshing, and gentle an environment as possible. Straighten any living areas and remove clutter from corridors and hallways. Consider opening the windows for a while if the weather is nice to let some fresh air into your home. This simple decluttering and clearing are in keeping with the popular idea that by establishing a clean, clear, and refreshing outer space, it will be easier to establish the same in your inner world. Have your timer and journal ready as well.

Stock Your Fridge

Make sure you have nourishing food at home so you don't have to go out. If you've had recipes in mind that you've wanted to make but haven't gotten around to them, it might be nice to make them during your retreat, so gather whatever ingredients you'll need. I like to stock a variety of fresh, leafy greens, other vegetables, and a variety of fruits, plus nut milk, turmeric, and tea for sipping on throughout the day. You can prepare any kind of food you like—so long as it is something you prepare and consume with intention and care. Try to avoid caffeine if you can.

Set Some Limits for the Day

In order to concentrate your focus on your practice, I recommend abstaining from the following habits that may be adding stress or distraction to your everyday routine:

- Television

- Phone

- Computer

- Smoking

- Alcohol

- Caffeine

If you feel nervous about being "cut off" from world events for a day, take a minute to breathe into that nervousness and perhaps investigate it a bit more by asking yourself if it is truly necessary to be "plugged in" every moment. Our culture teaches us to be constantly vigilant against missing information or opportunities (usually opportunities to buy things), and this can be one of the sources of stress in our daily lives. By consciously agreeing to let the outside world go by for just this one day, you add an extra element of cleansing, peace, and spaciousness to your life. Reassure your mind and body that you can always get caught up tomorrow; today is about meditation.

Practice Noble Silence

The term *noble silence* comes from the habit of the Buddha to remain silent when asked unanswerable questions. The idea is that by being mindful in keeping silent, we can better discern when speech is absolutely necessary. Keeping mindful silence means not only that you will not speak during your daylong retreat, but that you commit to being aware of any discomfort you may have with keeping silent, noticing any sudden urges to speak that do not come from absolute necessity, sitting with the feelings that may come up when resisting those urges, and investigating the root causes of those feelings.

Set a Schedule

The following is a suggested schedule for your day. You are welcome to make adjustments to it to accommodate your personal goals, but try to make sure that you are observing the intention of the retreat, which is to cultivate a deeper practice through meditating for longer periods of time over the course of an entire day. Before you begin your first session, be sure to eat breakfast so you are not distracted by hunger throughout the morning.

9:00–9:45: Seated Meditation

This time of seated meditation can be in whatever form you've established as your preferred "core" meditation practice. Settle into stillness and silence.

9:45–10:00: Walking Meditation

Review the section on walking meditation in chapter 3. In this meditation, while your body may be moving slowly and deliberately, your mind is resting in stillness and silence.

10:00–10:45: Seated Meditation

10:45–11:00: Walking Meditation

11:00–11:30: Journal Writing

Spend some time writing down any thoughts or feelings that came to you during your first two hours of meditation. It doesn't have to be anything monumental; you can start with "the sky is blue" and go from there. The goal is to free up your mind to write without judgment and really let your stream of consciousness flow onto the page and see where it leads. Write for yourself alone. Try to remain mindful as you write. Notice the sensation of the pen on the page, the sensations of your hand and arm as you write.

11:30–1:00: Make Lunch, Eat, Clean Up

Focus on making your meal without any distractions, and maintain noble silence. As you eat, pay attention to the sensations of eating—the textures, smells, tastes, as well as your environment. As you clean up, pay attention to the feel of the cups and plates in your hands, the warmth of the water, the texture of the sponge.

1:00–1:45: Seated Meditation

1:45–2:00: Walking Meditation

2:00–2:45: Seated Meditation

2:45–3:00: Walking Meditation

3:00–3:30: Break
Use this time for journaling, having a cup of tea, and maybe doing some light stretching.

3:30–4:15: Seated Meditation

4:15–4:30: Walking Meditation

4:30–5:00: Final Meditation

To formally end the retreat, take a few deep breaths. Sit and rest in the silence for a few moments, then place your hands over your heart and bow to yourself and the world around you in gratitude. You've given yourself a great gift!

You may want to spend some time with your journal to reflect on the day.

No train or plane tickets are necessary for you to experience a retreat-like environment. At the end of your retreat, you will have participated in over five hours of meditation! This is a big accomplishment. You can repeat this 1-day retreat as many times as you'd like. You may also wish to turn it into a 2-day retreat, perhaps adding some dedicated time to chant, sing, make music, or any other form of mindfulness that resonates with you. The most important piece here is that you have a clear plan and a dedicated end time and that you stick with it.

I encourage you to return to any or all of these meditation challenges whenever you feel your practice could use a boost. They can spice up your regular meditation practice and also help you get back on track if and when you feel you need it.

Afterword

A Zen master, on achieving enlightenment, found that he was able to understand true emptiness. One day, as he sat beneath a tree in a state of sublime silence, the tree began to shower him with flowers.

"We appreciate your lecture on emptiness," the gods said to him.

"But I have not said anything about emptiness," said the master.

"You have not said anything about emptiness, and we have not heard anything about emptiness," said the gods, "This is true emptiness."

And petals fell all around him like rain.

We all struggle, we all suffer. This is the human condition. Meditating like a Buddhist changes our relationship to suffering and to ourselves. It brings awareness, peace, and wellness beyond what we may have thought possible.

I've worked with all kinds of people in every situation imaginable: people experiencing profound loss, debilitating anxiety, depression, ADHD, insomnia, even just feeling a general sense of blah. Every person I've taught, even those who thought they wouldn't be able to meditate, could do it! Why? Because everyone has the ability to practice—we just convince ourselves otherwise.

The real block is that most of us are trying to escape our thoughts, which is why we overfill our days and, when there is a moment to rest, we numb out with food, spending, drugs and alcohol, or screens. At first, most of us are scared at what will come up if we put aside these numbing habits and start to sit with our thoughts and allow them to be as they are. Once we start, however, we quickly see there's no need to be afraid. We can change our relationship to our thoughts, our perspective, and the world becomes a different place. We feel safe and connected in this new world. We can see the beauty along with the hurt and the pain. There's no longer a need to be distracted, a desire to hide, or a feeling of being less than. There's no longer a pull to give ourselves to everyone and not care for ourselves. We see the value of expressing ourselves, no longer afraid of how others will respond. We feel open, trusting that all is working for our greatest good.

All this is yours for the taking.

The biggest thing to remember is that meditation is a practice, which means some days you're going to want to do it and other days you're not going to want to. Please be gentle with yourself. If you need to stop for a bit, make a plan for how and when you will come back. Know that you can always, always begin again. This book is full of recommendations about how and when to do this, but I encourage you to try the practice out and make it your own. If you have four kids and you're trying to figure out what a realistic amount of time to sit is, ask yourself how many minutes you have and that's your answer. Only you know how to make the practice doable for your particular circumstances, so that's your mission going forward. Meditation can work in so many places: sitting in your car, on a bench in the park, or waiting for your car to be serviced, at home or in the office. Please don't turn it into something that's untouchable and undoable, because you can only get the benefits if you actually do it.

Before you know it, the benefits of meditation will start finding you. Little things that might've derailed your day can now be taken in stride. Maybe you forgot your wallet in line at the store—instead of getting upset and berating yourself, you can simply notice you forgot it, put your items back, and walk out the door. Sure, you'll be annoyed for a second, but then you accept reality and move on with your day. You'll be around others and notice how rushed and harried they seem, and you'll deliberately slow down even more. You'll be in meetings or about to give a presentation and feel your heart pounding, and instead of psyching yourself up even more, you can close your eyes and do some deep breathing. You'll feel the benefits of meditation ripple out into every corner of your life, bringing ease, calm, and appreciation. No longer are you clinging to an invisible runaway horse—now you're taking the reins and enjoying the ride.

This is my wish for you. That you can take the practice of meditation and make it doable for you so that the benefits can flow into your life. Difficult emotions and situations won't just disappear from your life, any more than thoughts will disappear from your mind! But now, whenever you are experiencing worry, anxiety, stress, or fear, you'll recognize it as a cue for you to practice. The moment you begin your practice is the moment you come back to the present moment, leaving behind worries about the past and uncertainty about the future. As the present is all that we can control, your task is to come back to it again and again to remember that life is much larger than our worries make us believe. It's easy to become stuck in suffering, but you now have a practice to help you break free.

Acknowledgments

Being able to write this book was a true blessing for me. Meditation helped alleviate so much stress and anxiety in my life that if this introductory book can help you do the same, I'll be over the moon. I am extremely grateful to all of the teachers in my life who have helped guide and inform my practice. Their openness to share and serve is truly a blessing. It's important for me to shine a light on the McLean Meditation Institute where I deepened my practice and I learned to teach meditation and mindfulness to others.

Thank you to my brainstorming guru, S.S., and to I.L.N. for being such a sound voice for me throughout the book-writing process. And to my parents, sis, and in-laws for supporting and always showing interest in my work. While writing this book I was pregnant and gave birth! So I am extremely grateful to the Hierophant Publishing team for their patience and flexibility and caring for me and my words in such a kind way.

Lastly, I want to thank my husband and two baby loves; their presence is a constant reminder to care for my inner world so that I can love well and live with ease in my outer world.

About the Author

Cynthia Kane is the founder of the Kane Intentional Communication Institute, LLC and a certified meditation and mindfulness instructor. She teaches men and women how to change the way they communicate so they feel confident and present. She received her BA from Bard College and her MFA from Sarah Lawrence College. Her work has appeared in numerous publications, including the *Washington Post, Chicago Tribune, Yoga Journal, Self Magazine*, and *Woman's Day Magazine*. She is the author of *How to Communicate Like a Buddhist* and *Talk to Yourself Like a Buddhist*. Cynthia has helped over 40,000 people change their way of communicating through her online courses, workshops, and training program. She lives in Washington, DC with her main squeeze and two little loves. For more information go to http://cynthiakane.com.

Also from Heirophant Publishing

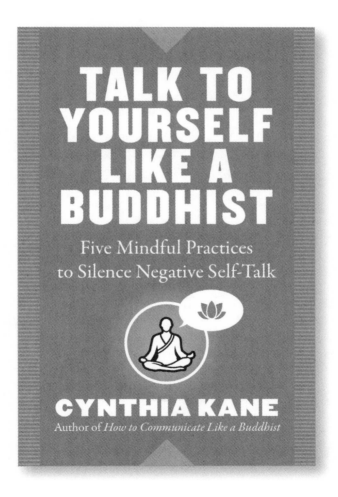

Available wherever books are sold.

Hierophant Publishing
8301 Broadway, Suite 219
San Antonio, TX 78209
888-800-4240

www.hierophantpublishing.com